LAOZI
TAO TE CHING
ON
THE ART OF HARMONY

LAOZI

TAO TE CHING

ON

THE ART OF HARMONY

THE NEW ILLUSTRATED EDITION
OF THE CHINESE PHILOSOPHICAL MASTERPIECE

TRANSLATED BY CHAD HANSEN

DUNCAN BAIRD PUBLISHERS
LONDON

The Art of Harmony
Translated by Chad Hansen

First published in the United Kingdom and Ireland in 2009 by
Duncan Baird Publishers Ltd
Sixth Floor, Castle House
75–76 Wells Street
London W1T 3QH

Conceived, created and designed by Duncan Baird Publishers

Managing Editor: Christopher Westhorp
Managing Designer: Daniel Sturges
Picture Research: Susannah Stone
Commissioned Calligraphy: Yukki Yaura

British Library Cataloguing-in-Publication Data:
A CIP record for this book is available from the British Library

ISBN: 978-1-84483-827-1

1 3 5 7 9 10 8 6 4 2

Typeset in Minion Pro
Colour reproduction by Colourscan
Printed in China by SNP Leefung Printers Limited

Notes:
Abbreviations used throughout this book:
AD Anno Domini (the equivalent of CE Common Era)
BC Before Christ (the equivalent of BCE Before the Common Era)
d. died

Prelim captions: Page 1 A 19th-century Taoist temple plate with *yin–yang* and trigram (*bagua*) symbols. **Pages 2–3** A Taoist temple at sacred Mount Wudang; (inset) a dragon-shaped jade pendant, Qing dynasty.

CONTENTS

Introduction 6

Tao Te Ching 36

AN INTRODUCTION
TO THE
TAO TE CHING

The *Daode Jing* (the *Tao Te Ching*, or the *Laozi*, translating as the *Classic of Ways and Virtues*) bewildered its audience from the moment it mysteriously emerged at the apex of classical Chinese thought in the third century BC. Laozi, its mythical author, was appropriated as a major voice in parts of the *Zhuangzi* (see pages 8–9), as a target of criticism for authoritarian Confucians and as an inspiration to despotic Legalists. Myths multiplied as his legend grew over two millennia. Was he the "missionary to India" who taught the Buddha what was to become Buddhism? Was he the God-like figure in the plethora of Daoist religions? Was he the ultimate master behind Chinese martial arts? Or was he the political revolutionary behind numerous popular rebellions against the empire? Each perspective sees itself somewhere in the text: Western missionaries found counterparts of God and creation myths; modern particle physicists have found, in Daoism's stunning naturalistic vision, deep insights into relativity and quantum mechanics; and science-fiction enthusiasts have found "the force" of *Star Wars*. What was really there? In ancient China, disputes about 道 *dao* had concerned the correct scheme for social harmony. The analysis presented in the *Laozi* turned people's imagination to a more inclusive harmony with nature.

The mysterious origins of the *Daode Jing* have spawned a rich field of text theories spanning three centuries, and best summarized in two stories. In the traditional tale, set in the sixth century BC, Confucius sought instruction from an archivist named Li Er 李耳 (styled "Dan" 聃) who had retired to live as a hermit. Later, Lao Dan (老聃 "Old Dan") left China, and as he was travelling west, a border guard asked him to "leave his *dao*". Old Dan obliged, quickly wrote out 5,000-plus characters, left China and disappeared. Popular later versions of the story placed him in India, where he either taught or became the Buddha – thus Daoism generated Buddhism.[1]

Old Dan was called Laozi (老子 "Old Philosopher", "Old Master") when associated with the short book of poetic wisdom left with the guard, which became known both as the *Laozi* and the *Daode Jing* (*Tao Te Ching*). Laozi was eventually deified in Daoist religion, and in the fourth century BC Zhuangzi (ca.365–285BC) studied the *Laozi* and elaborated the master's spiritual Daoism in his own much longer collection of stories and fables, the *Zhuangzi*.

The second story is set after Zhuangzi's death in the third century BC. Literarily gifted members of the Zhuangzi school engaged in the common Chinese practice of continuing to write in the style of their master (子 *zison*), embellishing and adding to the volume of related thoughts. Some of these superb stylists produced, in the form of the so-called "Outer" chapters of the *Zhuangzi*,[2] a cycle of fanciful dialogues between Confucius or his followers and Lao Dan or Laozi. In them, Lao Dan treats Confucius as naïve, dismissively criticizing his moral–political theories and ambitions from Zhuangzi's point of view. The dialogues all portray Confucius as humbly deferring to Old Dan's vastly superior wisdom.

At around this time, one or several writers (conceivably also from the school of Zhuangzi) set out to write (or compile from folk-sayings) a book which they (or others) then attributed to Laozi. The style is a four-character poetry rhythm from the *Book of Odes*[3] (a text Confucius had used in teaching and one of a handful thought to be older than the *Analects of Confucius* itself). These anonymous authors punctuate the four-character stanzas with a commentary-like six- or seven-character style of their own time, frequently introduced by a motif – 是以聖人 "therefore the sage. . ." – drawn from the pivotal second chapter of the "Inner" (perhaps original) chapters of the *Zhuangzi*. Other shared tropes found in both texts suggest the two text-writing groups were at least interacting while the *Laozi* and the "Outer" and "Miscellaneous" sections of the *Zhuangzi* took shape.

LOOKING FOR THE *LAOZI*

The search for an "original"

These two stories bracket many possible stories of the text's origin,[4] and for most of China's history some version of the first story had been accepted. It was formulated originally in a Han history, the *Shiji* 史記 (*Records of the Grand Historian*, ca.100BC), by Sima Tan and his son Sima Qian.[5] The father created the classification of "Daoism" and the son probably cobbled together the biography of Laozi, crediting him as the founder of Daoism. Both men were probably thinking of their own religion, the cult of Huang-Lao, a Legalist-leaning worship of Laozi alongside the mythical Yellow Emperor (Huang Di).

Textual studies in the nineteenth century began to introduce doubts and by the early twentieth century these were widespread among scholars. Gradually, the date of the *Laozi* began to match the second story. Scholarly reasoning drew on internal evidence – the style and content of the text – and external references and allusions to it. Recently, archaeological discoveries have confirmed the nineteenth-century doubters and suggest that many different copies of the text were circulating, being edited and augmented as late as the early Han period.[6]

There is no firm external evidence of the *Laozi*'s existence before about 250BC. When the first teachings did emerge, they drew immediate attention among philosophers. The *Xunzi* included an attack on Laozi and the first commentary is found in the *Hanfeizi*.[7]

The first of the archaeological finds consisted of two silk scrolls, called *Dao* and *De* (traditionally the first and second parts of the text). The *De* section is the more "political" and it was placed first, emphasizing a political focus. Later, a still earlier copy of a selection of chapters was discovered, one which followed (and thereby reinstated) the traditional order and was honed somewhat closer to the wording of the received text (by Wang Bi; see below). This confirmed that many copies must have been "in the evolutionary stream" and that the *De* scroll was still being augmented. The text against which everyone was comparing the finds was one by Wang Bi (AD226–249), edited after the collapse of the Han dynasty in AD220, who arguably drew on a range of surviving texts from this stream. Other extant reconstructions largely coincide with Wang Bi's. Guo Xiang (d.312) similarly edited the received text of the *Zhuangzi* and the Neo-Daoism (or "Dark Learning") movement brought Laozi and Zhuangzi back together (in that order) and joined them to the *Yijing* (*I Ching*, or *Book of Changes*).

A modern approach

The upshot of these evolving text theories is that we have no practical possibility of finding or reconstructing anything that would count as an original – in all likelihood Wang Bi was seeking the same thing. The search may be pointless. From its anonymous origins among multiple writers to its widespread popularity, its religious and political adoption, and its circulation in many different versions and collections, the text has been revised, edited and embellished over centuries. This should prompt only scepticism about any claims to have identified the "original" text.

The choice of a text, however, need not presuppose it is the original; there are other sound reasons for interpreting the familiar Wang Bi version – it allows one to compare the text with the hundreds of alternatives from many interpretive points of view – religious, philosophical, scientific, mystical and even "space fantasy". That traditional version combines a sparse elegance with the absence of editorial punctuation, titles, grammatical markers and other attempts to "guide" the reading toward the popular Qin and Han superstitions and later emerging religious movements. It even contains only one reference to the eclectic Confucian cosmology (*yin–yang* theory) that guided Wang Bi's own commentary and analysis.

Text scepticism shifts the focus from text theory to interpretation, though text theory still has a role identifying the relevant interpretive community and language. For this interpretation the community is the philosophical one in the wake of the "Inner" chapters of the *Zhuangzi*.[8] To understand a text in such a language it is necessary to survey the philosophical discussion and the lines of argument that would justify the *Laozi*, enabling a construction of the semantic meaning[9] of a text at that time and in that context. (Speculation about the attitudes and motivations of the various writers is a separate issue.)

PHILOSOPHY IN ANCIENT CHINA
Confucianism
The 論語, or *Analects of Confucius*, was like other classical texts in that it was a gradual accretion of writings by followers. Few doubt that Confucius (551–479BC) lived or that he originated some doctrines found in that text, but he wrote none of it. Many ideas and developments in the *Analects* probably came considerably later.

Confucius initiated the discussion with what is a remarkably natural and humanistic outlook. The most supernatural component was the school's appeal to the legitimizing authority of "sage kings" who, though incredibly wise, were still mortal human beings. They lived and died, leaving behind only their *dao*. Confucian veneration for these sages accompanies a less realistic conception of a golden age under their rule, but one guided by actual, transmitted norms of practice – 禮 or *li* ("ritual"). Confucius expressed a natural conception of 天 *tian* ("nature:sky", typically translated as "heaven"). *Tian's* main religious role was as a source of political legitimacy – the "Mandate of Heaven".

The ethical authority in the *Analects* is historical transmission from the originators of the practice of *li*. These conventional routines had been transmitted through successive generations, each committed to preserve, practise and teach this way of behaviour to the next generation. Their norms were grounded in transmission fidelity and loyalty to the sages. Compared to his Western counterparts, Confucius had an overwhelmingly sociological conception of ethics. He said he was a transmitter (of a ritual code), not a creator. Confucius used the concept 義 *yi* ("morality") but he did not openly contrast it to *li* as we would contrast morality and social mores.[10]

Confucius regularly paired the term *li* (禮) with *le/yue* (樂 "music/leisure: happiness"). This pairing, together with Mozi's later opposition (on the grounds of frugality), is explained by the insight that the stereotype of *le* ("music") was elaborate court entertainment, including orchestras, dancers and acrobats. *Li* and *le/yue* were social performances of a practised repertoire. Ritual performances similarly had a concert-like aspect, coordinating chanting and choreographed ritual steps.[11]

Confucius's model gave a different take on action. Learned ritual and musical performance both draw on how sound and rhythm "make us move" and help us to coordinate our movements with others in harmonious and aesthetic ways. That insight informs the baseline Confucian view of morality, *dao* and social life. When language eventually becomes an issue, the musical score-to-performance analogy continues to apply. Social discourse (language) is a means to coordinate social behaviour. Language plays a role analogous to that of ritual and music: it is tied to timing and the coordinated, harmonious joint performance of a practice.

The contrasting Western theory of action employed the logical notion of an argument, reasoning and inference. Aristotle's account of action treated beliefs and desires as premises in a practical form of deductive reasoning whose conclusion was a voluntary action.[12] This way of describing behaviour also breaks it up into units – actions – which became the focus of morality. The Confucian idea is more like that of a dance, a sequence of actions associated with a whole song – a *dao*. This became a background analogy for the later conception of the role of linguistic discourse.

The ancient Chinese viewed discourse as a crucial way of guiding behaviour – an ensemble social performance like *li*. The symbols making up the transmission encode techniques and moves for the different roles. The sages authored the codes and the classifications of roles that constituted the names/symbols in it. This was the recipe for the socially harmonious performance of the perfect society. The giving of roles was of a piece with the structure and the norms of behaviour. The details of how this worked were not made explicit. The focus was not on sentences (imperatives, assertions, desires, beliefs, duties, rights, principles) but names, individual words. The name was one's role or rank in a social ensemble and one was to "play one's part". Confucian ethics emphasized a person's role and the ritual behaviour that attached to it but the details, such as they were, were all in an obscure ritual "score" – the *Book of Li* – of social order, transmitted (in symbolic form) from the age of the sages.

This is known as the sage's *dao*, which the *Zhuangzi* and *Laozi* characterize as "human" *dao*. One's expression of duty can be judged for its pure correctness as well as for its aesthetic value, both as a performance of that role and as a participant in the harmonious symphony of social action. That was following a Confucian *dao*. People study, practise, internalize and eventually follow or perform a *dao* transmitted historically as *li* and *le* from the time it originated with the authoritative sage kings.

This core theory led to the Confucian political stance. Confucians thought

of government ideally as an educational or training structure with the ruler playing a role analogous to that of father in the family. The top of the hierarchy should have the greatest *de* (德 "virtuosity").[13] The ruler's work is not to pass laws, enforce or adjudicate them; he is simply to follow the rituals of his own role and model the kind of virtuosity in performance that we all should achieve in our respective social roles.

Thus the ruler resembles the player-conductor in an ensemble who sets the tone and pace of the performance. His second role is that of selecting the people to fill the next tier of leadership positions in the hierarchy. These people are chosen for their virtuosity in playing their role. Finally, in a theme that seems to emerge rather late in the text, he is to "rectify names".

Language became an issue in the Confucian system when they and rival thinkers focused on the details of training and guidance. Aesthetics may concern degrees of elegance and beauty in execution, but the issues of right and wrong persist. A score requires musicians to play certain notes in sequence or it does not count as a playing of the tune. A wrong note, however elegantly played, is not playing the piece correctly. Correctly following the score or ritual is applying or using its names correctly. One uses it correctly when one picks the right ritual artefact, role or behaviour.

Confucius addressed this issue in a late passage with a rare structure for the *Analects* – a *sorites* (paradoxical, little-by-little argument) leading from rectifying names to people knowing how to behave. The passage (13:3) argues that if names are not correctly used, the social system breaks down, *shi* (事 "affairs") dealings fail, ritual declines, the punishments miss their target and people don't know how to move their hands and feet. However, it offers no meta-analysis of what counts as right nor any way to show what is right. It simply concludes that the sage be "careful in his language". The sage teaches language by examples of use – by performing along with people. His use of words in the course of his ritual behaviour punctuates and guides his behaviour, just as singing and chanting would a dance. He makes utterances only where they are appropriately located in ritual performance. The deeper problem, however, applies to sages: how do they know what is right? What makes theirs a correct performance?

The *Analects'* eventual answer, a faculty of moral intuition called *ren* (仁 "humanity"), came to dominate Confucian thought. The *Analects* seems to envision this intuition as cultivated by training in and practise of *li*, which assumes our training and practice are themselves correct. Inept performance would generate an inept intuition. Even if the transmission from teacher to student were infallible, the question would remain of how the sages knew to initiate this particular traditional *dao*? And transmission does usually produce diversity. In languages the process leads to diffuse dialects or styles, not to a standard that is right. One dialect of Confucianism (the Mencius wing; see page 21) tried to solve the divergence problem by treating *ren* as innate. A tension between nature and nurture continued to plague Confucianism throughout its history.

Mohism

Mozi (Mo Di, ca.478–392BC), master of the rival moralist school called Mohism, advocated an impartial, utilitarian *dao*. His school appealed to the pragmatic outlook of skilled craftsmen, while Confucianism reflected the values of a quasi-priesthood of virtuosi in ceremonial ritual. Mozi parodied Confucian attachment to the traditional repertoire of ritual, particularly their dependence on employment as funeral mourners. The funeral ritual became a lightning rod for their dispute, which set the stage for a creative explosion in philosophical reflection.

The style of the *Mozi* was elaborate argumentative parallelisms[14] in contrast to the *Analects'* pithy aphorisms. Rhythm and timing carried the heart-mind's thinking as music carried the body. This probably aided in oral memory as well as in clarifying argument and syntactic structure. This contrast and their intense opposition to Confucian *dao* concealed many shared assumptions which later motivated Zhuangzi to pair them.

Mozi agreed that the role of a political structure was to provide a score, a single guiding discourse that could harmonize social behaviour. His focus was just as social, but with a more explicit role for language. Social *dao* is the entire body of ongoing discourse that greases our *shi*. This made it obvious that cultural history is a circular standard in selecting and reforming this social discourse. Mohists still contemplated a social hierarchy of virtuosity and agreed that harmony grew out of people using words (名 *ming* "names") in similar ways.

Both Confucius and Mozi were naturalistic. Humans are creatures who inherit standards and ways of acting from their elders and superiors. However, Mozi broadened the legitimizing role of *tian* (天 "nature:sky") from politics to norms in general. *Tian* replaced the historical sage kings as the authority that chooses and interprets social *dao*. *Tian*'s standard for judging social *dao*s, Mozi argued, is a *li-hai* (利 害 "benefit–harm") distinction. He tried to prove that empirically by finding evidence of *tian*'s *zhi* (志 "ambition") in the natural patterns that benefit human life. For him, evidence of design did not argue for an intelligent creator, but for an inherent, goal-like structure in natural process. All natural kinds are guided by a *li-hai* distinction. Nature makes benefit available for creatures, thus endorsing and rewarding their natural inclination. People learn most of their values from a transmitted, malleable tradition, but they need no instruction to prefer benefit over harm. So Mozi's natural standard for the correct social *dao* was general human utility. The right way to talk and engage in *shi* is the way that impartially benefits everyone. His proposed reforms included simplifying burial practices and government frugality, centred on eliminating Confucius's elaborate ceremonial *le*.

Mozi's utilitarianism did not focus on acts or rules, but on the entire social *dao*. Mozi used argument, but did not rely on any rational end. A natural *bian* (辯 "distinction") guides human social engineering of their *dao* – Mozi is an ethical naturalist. *Tian* has the Western religious role of being a source of legitimacy for *dao*s, but not of making them supernatural. Norms are built into the natural structure of the world, in natural processes.

Besides normative naturalism, *tian* introduces an emphasis on *chang* (常 "constancy"); the reliability, neutrality, and universality of *dao*. Different regions, the passage of time, and a plurality of interpretive points of view all affect traditional norms. As Mozi noted, if people do not like the *dao* in a region, they can leave; they cannot as easily escape the domain of *tian*. If the norms of two traditions conflict, only a naturally operational *fa* (法 "standard") – for example a *li-hai* distinction – can tell us which is right, or how to reform our own. People need some way to know which tradition and which hierarchy of models to follow – which play or which concerto to perform. They can play together only if they agree on a tune and a standard for judging correct playing and virtuosity. This natural focus shifted Mozi's attention from ritual and inherited social mores to a recognizable conception of objective morality.[15] The Mohists came to see tradition as one of three standards of correct language use, but the core legitimacy of *dao* rests on the third, the neutral, universal and operationally determinate distinction of *li-hai*.

This led Mozi to an important contribution to Daoism – the idea of a constant *dao* (道 "guide") based on a "constant" *yan* (言 "language"). A constant *dao* is one that works for all cultures, benefits all humans, and gives objective, reliable guidance. Its interpretation should be transparent to ordinary people using only their eyes and ears and need no further reform.

Mozi's political mechanism for reform starts from the bottom: someone (say a craftsman) using the *li-hai* standard discovers the *shi* (是 "this:right") way to do something, and he conveys it up the hierarchy. In this view, government works more like a universal judicial appeal system than a scheme of legislation and enforcement. Each higher authority either confirms or overturns lower *shi-fei* (是非 "this–not this") judgements and everyone abides by the resulting scheme. If upheld by higher levels in the evaluative hierarchy, including the supreme *tian zi* (*tian* master) who defers to *tian*'s authority by using the benefit–harm distinction, and if it benefits the whole society impartially, Mozi said to make that discourse "constant" (常之 *chang zhi* "constant it"). Spread it throughout the social world and preserve it over generations. This process of harmonizing practical judgements gives Mozi his distinctive mechanism for using utility in morality and completes the ideal of a constant *dao* (道 "guide").

Humans can reliably follow a constant social *dao* – its interpretation is as constant as its structure. Humans are guided not only by the practices of their elders and superiors, but by the terms (名 *ming* "names") that constitute their social *dao*s. A social way of using language that emphasizes partiality to family (as Confucianism does) will make people partial in their behaviour; a language that emphasizes neutral universality will make people more egalitarian in their behaviour; and so on.

The *Mozi* presents three *fa* (法 "standards") of the correct use of language. The first is conformity with past usage, going back to the sage kings. The second targets the Confucian reliance on the cultivated intuition of the elite (君子 *junz* "superior men"): the standard should be applicable by ordinary people. The crucial third standard dominates Mozi's examples: it is the utility of guiding behaviour using language this way. Mozi relies mostly on this standard to order his socially engineered linguistic *dao*.

Whereas in the Western model law governed people's private choices, Chinese thought addressed the apparatus of choice (the language or discourse) so that people operate on the same norms and guided by a single, unified scheme of concepts – a single, constant *dao*. This is why, despite bitter disagreement on the content of that *dao*, Zhuangzi paired Confucians and

Mohists and made them his joint target. Both advocate unifying the social world with a single scheme of guidance – a single social *dao*.

Mozi's development of this approach led to the intense focus on language that characterizes the mature period of Chinese philosophy. The *Laozi* echoes with the language themes, but rarely employs the technical terms. The *Laozi* wrestles with the role of language in claims about *dao*, the contrast of social tradition versus natural process, and the analysis of *wei* (為 "deeming action").

Mencius and other views fuelling "Laoism"

Mencius (Mengzi, ca.385–305BC), a Confucian who responded to Mozi, acknowledged the Mohist point that *yi* (see page 12) is not merely conventional social practices; that it rests on some neutral ground. He also found that ground in *tian*, but argued that *tian* endowed humans with a more complex set of moral attitudes and intuitions. These are embedded in the physical structure of our *xin* (心 "heart-minds"). The operation of these innate responses, he suggested, grew into Confucian norms just as seeds grow into mature plants. The natural development of these inborn moral attitudes results in a "cultivated" *xin* that makes accurate situational *shi-fei* judgements, of which those made by cultivated *junz* naturally harmonize in the expression of conventional Confucian virtues. Conventional mores, thus, are a result, rather than a cause, of human moral dispositions. Mencius put the intuition of *ren* as the first among his four *xin*, making access to particular situational *shi-fei* judgements again a matter of cultivated intuition.

Mencius claimed he was forced to engage in *bian* (辯 "distinction dispute") by the doctrines both of Mozi and Yang Zhu (ca. fourth century BC). Yang was an ethical egoist whose position has to be reconstructed from fragments. He is often associated with "primitivism", modelled on hermits who shunned society, social values and public life. Like Mencius and Mozi, Yang grounded his ethical norms in a *tian dao* but he thought that being natural required a rejection of all social *dao*s because they interfere with the orientation and flow of natural energies toward self-interest. Following natural *dao* was following a *dao* of *wo* (我 "I:me"). Primitivism's point of departure is that any social norm structure interrupts the natural flow and distorts the spontaneous or instinctive reactions to situations. This ethos was first evident in the *Analects* through accounts of hermits who confront Confucius as the *Zhuangzi* authors imagined Lao Dan would have.

A little-known thinker included in the internal *Zhuangzi* history of thought between the Mohists and Laozi, Song Xing (360–300BC) emphasized how linguistic and evaluative attitudes reflect rather than validate social ways of using language. Our natural desires, he said, are few and simple. The desires cultivated by absorbing a tradition multiply without limit and lead to competition and strife. This insight is developed beautifully in the *Laozi*.

The *Zhuangzi* history places another group between the Mohists and Laozi – one centred around Shen Dao (390–315BC). Shen Dao constructed a concept of a *da-dao* (大道 "great way"), which is the actual course of the past and future history of everything. Then he observed that we always have followed, are following and always will follow Great *Dao*. People can relax and do not need to study or learn what to do. Even a clod of earth cannot miss Great *Dao*. His slogan was "abandon knowledge and discard 'self'" – that is, abandon even *yang*'s egoist *dao*. Relax and flow and you will follow Great *Dao* whatever you do.

THE *LAOZI*

The theory of opposites

The *Laozi* builds its philosophy around Shen Dao's "abandon knowledge" slogan but it does not depend on Shen's implicit "fatalism". Its reasoning reflects primitivism but without Yang Zhu's emphasis on a *dao* of *wo*. Like Song Xing, it analyzes knowing as internalizing some social *dao*, maybe Confucius's

or Mozi's, but treats it as enslavement by that social *dao*, not mastery of something of natural worth. The enslavement is subtle and insidious because it consists in instilling socially constructed desires that conflict with our natural desires and impulses. The *Laozi* elegantly pulls this all together in its theory of language, names, desires and *wei* (為 "deeming action" – acting on social constructs).

The *Laozi*'s hallmark is the view that names (guiding terms in a social *dao*) come in pairs, like *mei* (美 "beautiful") and *e* (惡 "ugly"). They are learned together as a contrast (just as children's books teach "over" and "under"). Each pair forms one system pivoting around a single distinction – if it is beautiful, then it is not ugly. That resembles a constant *dao*, but it doesn't tell you where to draw the distinction between the opposites. Each transmitted, learned scheme deploys a different distinction point. What counts as moral to a Confucian is immoral to a Mohist and vice versa. Learning their language biases us to see reality as being divided in their way. Nature doesn't draw those distinctions.

The first (*Dao*) section of the *Laozi* avoids the analytic terms developed by Mohists that feature in Mencius's and Zhuangzi's outlooks (*bian*[16] and *shi-fei*). They emerge, but without stress, in the more political second (*de*) section. The *Laozi*'s distinctive addition to the Confucian and Mohist view of language as guiding behaviour, and the analysis of the mechanism as term distinctions and opposites, is that the scheme of opposites shapes our *yu* (欲 "desires"), our values. Consequently, a whole socially constructed *dao* guides our behaviour. *Wei* (為 "deeming action") is having our behaviour guided by deeming something to be on one side or the other of these social distinction points. In learning to class something as "beautiful", one learns to perceive it as having value, to want it and to disvalue its opposite, *e* (惡 "ugly", pronounced "ugh!").

Language as a social-control mechanism thus determines not only how people see difference, but which side people desire. When we act on that socially constructed desire, it is called *wei* (為 "deem:acting"). To give up *wei*-ing (無 *wu* "lack", 為 *wei* "deem:do") is thus to give up the social *dao* – the community's names, its socialized ways of making distinctions (concepts), the instilled desires, and any behaviour conditioned by them.

Since the interlocking system of linguistic control interferes with our natural flow, the key to liberation from it is forgetting the names that lie at its base. If we erase the names from our behaviour-guiding mechanism, we can revert to natural ways of making distinctions and choosing courses of action. We lose *learned* desires for social goods and we keep natural desires, natural values. Social goods include things such as money, status, rare objects, fine wines, perfumed body parts, stylish clothes and decorative surroundings. They are enslavements which we do not value spontaneously but because others value them. Social values are a normative Ponzi scheme.

The *Laozi* implicitly acknowledges the obvious difficulty of *forgetting* our language distinctions and pursues an indirect strategy. Zhuangzi emphasized the relativity of opposite values and guidance. The *Laozi* draws attention to the relativity with a heuristic device: *fan* (反 "reversal"). Reversing opposites is treating what is conventionally valued as a non-value to reveal a still viable *dao*. The examples, drawn from folk wisdom, employ universally powerful metaphors that enrich the text and make the *Laozi* so popular. What do we learn when we learn that our traditional scheme of guiding concepts can be enhanced by reversal? The *Laozi*'s opening thesis: *dao*s that can guide us are not constant.

Rhetorically the *Laozi* sometimes sounds close to Buddhism, but Buddhism rejects natural desires – notably sexual desire – while Daoism celebrates sexuality. It combines this open-mindedness with its *fan* emphasis on femininity in ways that can challenge translators to stay within the bounds of decency and fuels a later Daoist fascination with sexual practices, which may partially account for its popularity.

Natural desires, those needing no learning or training, are few and simple. This implicit acceptance of one's self-nature contrasts with Christian self-hate and Buddhist renunciation,[17] and it underlies Daoism's appeal to psychological theorists. Even the *Laozi*'s opprobrium for society disappears in Zhuangzi's mature Daoism, which accepts human society and language as themselves natural while emphasizing the relativity of social conceptions of "right" and is sceptical that any small corner of the world has got it right.

THE KEY CONCEPTS OF DAOISM

Introduced here are some key terms from the *Laozi*, with the translation explained and some alternatives presented. This should help the reader to appreciate the difficulty of translation and why interpretations of the text can vary so widely. The terms are arranged in order of importance (*dao* first) and an effort has been made to keep related terms and compounds close together.

道 *dao* ("guide")

The simple translation is "way". The grammatical differences in "way" and *dao* are harder but are important. *Dao* can be used as a verb in Chinese – the activity of *dao*s, "to guide". *Dao* resists individuation; any *dao* consists of *dao*s and is part of some larger *dao*. A way from one point to another can consist of a web of alternate choices of nodes and links. Each link can count as a way and a collection of links or paths can also count as a way. The worldwide web is a *dao*.

Conveniently, Chinese common nouns do not have individuation built in. They neither take plural forms nor combine with articles to form noun-phrases. They behave rather like a blend of plurals and proper names (hence their use of 名 *ming*/"names" of designating terms in general). *Dao* has a grammar that is like "water" or "wood" but is not, like these, a *wu* (物 "thing-kind"), hence lacks a *ming*.

The ubiquitous "the" in other translations of *dao* is always added by the translator. This translation has opted for indefinite reference (a/some *dao*) or uses the plural (*daos*) and reserves singular form for modified *dao* (for example, my father's *dao* = the sum of my father's *daos*).

The even more difficult question is defining or explaining ways/*daos*. What kind does it belong to? One candidate answer is that a *dao* answers a "how" question. *Daos*, however, can also tell us categorically what *to* do. *Daos* are what we seek when we wonder what to do. The concept of *dao* is broader than "morality" and encompasses norms of all types: legal *daos*; prudential *daos*; fashion *daos*; scientific, linguistic and epistemological *daos*.

It is easier to make a list of subtypes of *dao*/way than to analyze it. That list includes procedures, paths, instructions, plans, practices, sequences of events or processes, histories, maps and even lines and arrows. Computer programs are *dao* and a computer's hard-wired operating system is a *dao*.

Dao-based behaviour typically has two phases: choice of a guiding *dao* and the performance-interpretation of it. To understand the second, think of how we use "interpretation" to evaluate a player's performance of a musical piece. Interpretation is not a theory but an execution of the guide. When we walk down a path we read the markings to guide our steps. We interpret guiding *dao*-structures as we do plays and songs – in an actual performance of them. Both phases contribute to the puzzle of individuation – there are *dao* of choosing *dao*, which we "perform-interpret" when we choose some guidance structure. Similarly, there are *daos* of following, interpreting *daos*. Both these *dao* of *dao* are both chosen and interpreted. The two phases give *dao* an even more complex structure and make it more puzzling how to individuate them.

The most familiar alternate translation for *dao* is "road" or "path." A road is a *dao* in three dimensions, a map is a *dao* in two dimensions, a single arrow or pointing finger is a one-dimensional *dao*. A way of behaviour adds the fourth – time – dimension. The relations between these is like the relation between a guiding *dao* and an interpretive or choice *dao* – a map represents a road which represents a way to get to our goal. Space–time contexts for *dao* explain why modern physicists, as well as psychologists, find fascination in Daoism. And it can help us explain the metaphysics of *dao*. They are space–time structures.

Space–time – the path of light rays – is shaped by the distribution of force/matter. *Dao*s are not forces or things, but are the result of the placement of things (trees, rocks, swamps). They are opportunities or openings for action by some creature, so *dao*s are relative to potential *dao*-walkers. The way for a professional skier to get through a difficult run amid the trees is not the way for a forty-year-old beginner. That is why *dao*s are everywhere and endless – for every *dao* there are ways of choosing it and ways of interpreting/performing it and ways of choosing/interpreting those and so on, *ad infinitum*.

大道 *Da-dao* ("Great Dao")

If we assimilate the entire scope of *dao*s to a single cosmic "performance *dao*", we can call that Great *Dao*. Great *Dao* would be the entire history of everything from the Big Bang to the featureless fizzle we are destined to become.

天道 *Tian-dao* ("natural *dao*")

Natural *dao* is not all that happens, but more like all guidance structures produced by *constant* natural processes. Hard determinism identifies Great *Dao* with *tian-dao*, but if natural causal processes are not deterministic, the same natural *dao* could be consistent with many possible Great *Dao*s. Zhuangzi argued that neither Great *Dao* nor natural *dao* could be a guiding *dao* because we have no possibility of misperforming them or choosing wrong. The *Laozi* tends to valorize natural *dao* as a guide. Zhuangzi regards all existing, rival *dao*s as natural in the sense that their advocacy and existence in any community is a consequence of the operation of natural processes.

天 *tian* ("nature:sky")

Some suspect *tian* may once have been a divinity – even anthropomorphic – but by the start of classical philosophy its naturalization was nearly complete. The religious reminder is its legitimating role – the "Mandate of Heaven" legitimizing rulers and the neutral authority legitimizing the rival social *daos* of Confucian, Yangist and Mohist moralists. Within nature, *tian* consists of the *dao* that are *chang* (常 "constant") – like the paths of the sun, moon and stars. One formula for Daoism is that Daoists deny that *tian* (天 "nature:sky") can play that normative role unless there is a *tian-dao* (天道 "natural dao") – all normative authority must stem from a *dao*, not from nature as a thing.

天地 *Tian-di* ("heaven and earth")

Many Chinese concepts are formed by joining opposite terms. Combining "heaven-earth" produces a term to refer to the cosmos. In the translation "cosmos" is preferred to "world" to preserve the distinction with *tian-xia*.

天下 *Tian-xia* ("below-heaven")

The fundamental dichotomy of Chinese thought is not appearance versus reality but social versus natural. In this translation *tian-di* is the natural world, *tian-xia* is "the social world". The latter is preferred to the usual "the empire" because, firstly it is not a political term but a positional one, and secondly because the text is located before the empire had come into being (its scope at the time of writing would include all the warring states and perhaps even "barbarians").

為 *wei* ("deem:do")

Action in the *dao*-model revolves around *wei* (為 "deem:do"). A social *dao*, for example Confucian *li* (禮 "ritual"), is a string of words.[18] These guide action by guiding how we select and reject things in our environment. We assign a word to these things implicitly or explicitly. Intending or acting in a certain way casts that thing in the role marked by the word in the guiding text. The related term *wei* (謂 "call") is used when we do this explicitly or call attention to how to assign the word. *Wei* has been translated here as "acting on (social) constructs".

以為 *yi-wei* ("deem:act")

The *wei* thus plays a role in the nearest Chinese counterpart of Western beliefs: *yi* (以) with some item X we "deem:act" on some concept Y. This is to regard and treat something in the situation as being of a type or under some classification. Deeming can be expressed or entailed by behaviour (one mode is speech or writing). When we *wei*, we assign something to a role in our social *dao*. There is a short form of the *yi-wei* complex that is important in the *Laozi*. It uses Y as the main transitive verb and X as the verb's object – as in "to befriend someone" is to deem-make them a friend. A belief is thus a *dao* of behaviour associated with a term and some contextual object.

為天下 *wei tian xia* ("deem:act on the social world")

Wei (為 "deem:do") may be used with a central guiding concept from some social *dao*. Yang Zhu's *dao* would be described as *wei-wo* (為我 "deem:act on me/I") and the Mohist *dao* as *wei-gong* (為公 "deem:act on the public"). Deem-acting on the whole social world would be the guiding conception of the impartial sage – but it has a hint of paradox because this presupposes some social discourse *dao* to which we conform when we *wei* (為 "deem: do"). Further, if the conception of taking the sage's guiding point of view is inventing the social-guiding discourse for the world (as the sages allegedly did), then this is to take an inherently unequal, paternalistic ethical stance. One must presuppose some *dao* that is prior to any social-guiding discourse to justify such a moral presumption.

知 *zhi* ("know")

The modern Chinese translation of "know" is *zhi* (知 "know") *dao* (道 "guide"), and knowing in ancient China was related to *wei*-ing – *wei*-ing correctly or successfully. However, we can know objects, names, how to combine, and consequently what to do. The *Laozi* sometimes condemns *zhi* (conventional constructs to be abandoned) but at other times recommends *knowing*; for example, how to free oneself from conventions. The same duality applies to its treatment of sages – sometimes urging us to dispense with them and at other times appealing to their authority. The ambiguity applies with a vengeance to *wei*-ing. In recommending against it, we are doing it. Laozi inherits this prescriptive paradox from Shen Dao's slogan "abandon knowledge" – if we follow it we disobey it. Since the *Laozi* elaborates on that advice, an air of paradox lingers in many of its epistemic terms. Hence we must know not to know, must not *wei* and yet not not *wei*.

明 *ming* ("discern")

This translation has been chosen to emphasize the *dao*-based context – being able to perceive the distinctions we use to act on *dao*s. *Ming* (明 "discerning") also is rarely negative because it allows us to perceive both social and natural distinctions. Typically, layering social distinctions over the natural ones interferes with spontaneous *ming* (明 "discernment").

聖人 *sheng-ren* ("sages")

Confucianism credits these quasi-divine ancients as the inventors of the Confucian social, ritual *dao*, and Mohists countered with still earlier authorities. This gives sages an ambivalent role in the *Laozi*: as examples of what should be abandoned – along with knowledge, language, and acting on social constructs – but also as models of the resulting correct natural behaviour. It can frequently be puzzling whether the oft-repeated sage commentary illustrates the correct point or shows how presumptuous authorities misinterpret or make arbitrary choices to impose on the rest of us.

善 *shan* ("good-at")

In a *dao* context, good – like belief, knowledge, and so on – has a practical use: being good *at* something, mastery. It can be mastery of applying a construct, a role or achieving some real goal in nature.

德 *de* ("virtuosity")

This is what is achieved when a person internalizes some *dao*, learns and practises it. *De* governs the quality of our performance. "Virtuosity" as a translation emphasizes the aesthetics of performing *dao*, rather than a two-valued, right–wrong. The normal translation as "virtue" is acceptable if it is understood, in the Aristotelian sense, as "excellence". "Virtuosity" is preferred because "virtue", with its overtones of sexual chastity, retains familiar Christian moralistic overtones that would rupture the crucial conceptual link to the aesthetic model. Further, "virtue" does little (without supernatural intervention) to incorporate Arthur Waley's insight that "power" is a component of the meaning of *de*. Virtuosity explains overtones of power arising from a reliable ability to execute one's *dao* correctly and elegantly – hence a virtuoso boxer can beat a muscle-bound bruiser. Those with virtuosity naturally come to be regarded as leaders, models and teachers.

常 *chang* ("constant")

Mozi associates *chang* with *tian*, whose *dao* is unchanging. By contrast, human *dao*s are subject to interpretive variability because they use *yan* (言 "language"). Mozi thought a *dao* guided by *li-hai* would be constant in two senses: it would be interpretively fixed, and it would never require revision over time. The *Laozi* opens with a ringing formulation of the impossibility of

Mozi's goal: any *dao* that can guide is not constant because the interpretation of names cannot be fixed. The *Laozi* uses *chang* in the verb position (see *yi-wei*, page 30) and the translation given here renders these as "fix on" and "concentrate on" as well as the conventional "constantly".

物 *wu* ("thing-kinds")

Wu contrasts with *shi* (事 "affairs") to reflect the Chinese philosophical dialectic of nature versus society. *Wu* are natural kinds, and like other common nouns it does not pluralize, so while "thing" (the common translation) works, "thing-kind" is more accurate if we remember they are concrete objects (*concreta*).

萬物 *Wan-wu* ("10,000 thing-kinds")

The routine use of this number reminds us that *wu* are not particulars. Even a quick survey would convince us there are 10,000 stars alone and far more grains of sand. The term is often used to refer to living species (usually animals) and, roughly, is the real counterpart of any *ming* (名 "names"), or designating term in general.

器 *qi* ("utensil:implement")

Qi are things that play roles in human life – tools – and which thus fall on the social side of the social–natural dialectic to contrast with *wu* (物 "natural-kinds"). This translation mostly avoids "thing" in favour of "implement" or "utensil".

氣 *qi* ("life-force")

Qi is in some sense like "matter" as the ultimate constituent stuff, but it excites modern physicists because it connotes "energy" or "force". It is conventionally used of the life-force, the breath, that animates living things until it is exhausted.

名 *ming* ("names")

All terms seem to be regarded as *ming* (名 "names") and the best explanation probably lies in the lack of pluralization for Chinese nouns. They function, as proper names, plurals and mass nouns do, without required articles to form complete noun phrases. Adjectives and intransitive verbs can do this as well, although there is a linguistic distinction (in the choice of negations). All were associated with a scope or range *named* by the term. Retaining "name" as the translation has the advantage of reminding the reader that Chinese theory of language is nominalist: conventional terms (sounds or visual characters) denote and refer without any mediating ideas or forms.

言 *yan* ("language")

Yan can sometimes be translated as "speech", at other times as "doctrine". The full theoretical breadth is captured best by the more general translation "language" or "discourse".

事 *shi* ("affairs")

Social things, affairs, dealings, are all things whose existence depends on humans and their social practices and attitudes. So schools, offices, teachers, officials, laws, and so on would be just brick, human protoplasm and wood pulp if there were no human practices in which they played roles. Human practices rely on a shared and mutually acknowledged framework for dealing with others. Natural kinds, by contrast, would exist whether or not humans had evolved or formed societies.

自然 *zi-ran* ("self-so")

The compound traditionally translated as "nature" is formed of 自 ("from/self") and 然 ("so-thus"), hence "that-which-is-so-of-itself" without the addition of social structures, institutions and practices. The advantage of translating it as "self-so" is both to mark a distinction from *tian* (天 "nature:sky") and the Mencian concept of *xing* (性 "nature"), which does not play much role in the *Laozi*, and to emphasize the local-perspective relative focus in the *Zhuangzi*.

有 無 *you-wu* ("exist–not exist")

These are Chinese concepts of existence which also function as transitive verbs (have/lack). This makes them different from Western concepts, which function as linking verbs, so that existence gets bound up with a thing's properties and essence. The problem posed in Chinese arises from treating these as *ming* (名 "names") where the nominalism is cast in terms of distinctions. The issue is: in what *reality* do the opposites *you-wu* (有 無 "exist–not exist") mark a distinction? Whatever the distinction separates off as *wu* should also be described as *you*. If *wu* is a name and names something other than *you*, that something it names must exist. There must be that something which *wu* names. This is the famous puzzle of the first chapter that eventually becomes the central puzzle of Neo-Daoism and Buddhism.

TAO
TE CHING

1

DAOS, NAMES
AND PUZZLES

Ways can be guided; they are not fixed ways.
Names can be named; they are not fixed names.
"Absence" names the cosmic horizon,
"Presence" names the mother of 10,000 natural kinds.
Fixing on "absence" is to want to view enigmas.
Fixing on "presence" is to want to view phenomena.
These two, emerging together, we name differently.
Conceiving of them as being one: call that "fathomless".
Calling it "fathomless" is still not to fathom it.
. . . the door to a cluster of puzzles.

有
無
相
生

2

LANGUAGE AND CONTRASTS

When all the social world regards beauty as "beauty",
Here already is "ugly".
If all treat mastery as "being good at" things,
Here already is "not being good at" things.
Thus "presence" and "absence" mutually sprout.
"Hard" and "easy" mutually inform.
"Long" and "short" are mutually gauged.
"High" and "low" mutually incline.
"Sound" and "tone" mutually blend.
"Before" and "after" mutually follow on.
Using this: sages don't act on constructs in addressing affairs;
They practise a "don't-use-language" teaching.
10,000 natural kinds are made by it
Yet don't express anything.
Sprouting, you don't treat them as "existing".
Acting on constructs, you don't rely on anything.
Success taking form, you don't dwell on it.
In general, they simply don't dwell on it,
And in that, they don't lose it.

3

ARTIFICIAL DESIRES

Don't elevate the outstanding:

Then your subjects will not contend.

Don't value hard-to-get goods:

Then your subjects will not act as thieves.

Don't display the desirable:

Then your subjects' minds will not be muddled.

Using these: The way a sage maintains order:

Empties their minds,

Stuffs their guts,

Weakens their resolve,

And strengthens their bones.

He fixes on making his subjects lack both knowing and desiring.

Makes the wise not presume to act on constructs.

Act on the construct "lack acting on constructs".

Then nothing is not ordered.

淵
兮
似
萬
物
之
宗

4

REFLEXIVE
DAOS

Ways permeate, but in using them
Part remains unfilled.
Oh! Deep! . . . Like the ancestor of 10,000 natural kinds.
Treat what they make "sharp" as "dull"
Treat what they make "tied" as "loose"
Treat what they make "bright" as "blurred"
Treat what they make "dust" as "together".
Oh! Profound! . . . Like they partly exist.
I don't know whose offspring they are.
They predate the lord of signs.

天
地
不
仁

5

NATURE'S INDIFFERENCE

The cosmos is not humane.

It treats 10,000 natural kinds as straw dogs.

Sages are not humane.

They treat the people as straw dogs.

Is the space between heaven and earth (the cosmos)

Not like a bellows pipe?

Emptying, it doesn't warp.

Moving, it produces more.

Much discourse, counting to the limit,

Best to stay near the middle.

6

THE NATURAL CREATIVE POWER

The valley's spirit never gives out.
This is called "the fathomless female".
The gate of the fathomless female:
This is called "the source of the cosmos".
Silken! It's as if it exists.
In using it, relax.

不
自
生

7

SELF-FOCUS

The sky is old and the earth is enduring.
The reason the cosmos can survive and endure is that
   it avoids self-creation.
Hence they can be old and enduring.
Using this: sages, in putting their being last,
Their being comes first.
In treating their being as outside,
Their being exists.
Is this not their lacking self-focus
So they can give their self-focus form?

上善若水

8

BEING GOOD AT THINGS

Advanced mastery is like water.

Water, good at benefitting 10,000 natural kinds, doesn't contend.

Where it settles repels the human crowd.

Hence it is *close* to paths.

In dwelling, master "the land".

In mentality, master "depth".

In associations, master "humanity".
In discourse, master "accuracy".
In correcting, master "ordering".
In dealings, master "possibility".
In activity, master "timing".
In general, simply don't contend
Thus avoid criticism.

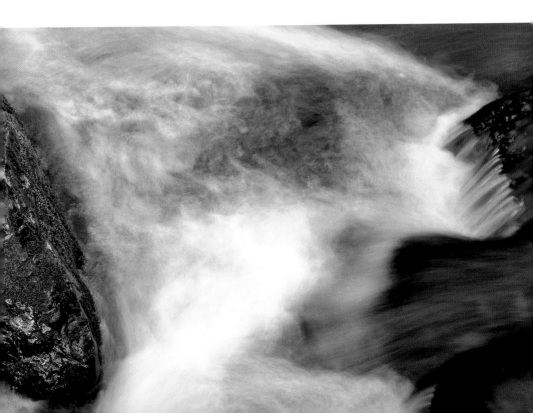

揣而銳之不可長保

9

GETTING VERSUS ACHIEVING

Grasping, we fill it up.
It is better to let it be.
Measuredly, you sharpen it;
You cannot preserve the edge for long.
When gold and jade fill the hall,
We can't preserve any of it.
Being rich and valued, we are proud.
The error of self-destruction!
When success flows, retreat:
This is a natural way.

10

UNFATHOMABLE VIRTUOSITIES

In general: in mustering your vitalities,
Enveloping them as one,
Can you avoid distinguishing?
In concentrating life-force and making it supple,
Can you be a child?
Polishing your unfathomed vision,
Can you eliminate all flaws?
In loving the nation and putting the subjects in order,
Can you avoid acting on constructs?
In opening and closing the heavenly channel,
Can you act the female role?
In discerning all within the four directions,
Can you lack know-how?
Generate it, nourish it:
Generating it we don't treat it as "present".
Acting on constructs, we don't rely on them.
Becoming "elder" we don't preside.
These are called "unfathomable virtuosities".

11

VALUING ABSENCE

Thirty spokes join one hub.
The cart's use lies where they are absent.
Throwing clay to make a vessel;
The vessel's use lies where the clay is absent.
Sculpting windows and doors to make a room;
The room's use lies where they are absent.
So we treat having something as beneficial and treat lacking
  something as useable.

為
腹
不
為
目

12

PRACTICES AND SPONTANEITY

Five colours stupefy human eyes.
Five tones desensitize human ears.
Five flavours numb human mouths.
Horse racing and hunting derange human minds.
Hard-to-get goods pervert human behaviour.
Using this: sages act for the belly,
Not the eye.
And so discard "that" and take up "this".

13

SOCIAL APPROVAL AND VALUE

Favour is as disgraceful as a warning.
Value your calamities as part of your being.
Why say "favour is as disgraceful as a warning"?
Bestowing favour is treating you as lower.
Receiving favour is like a warning.
Losing it is like a warning.
This is why I say "favour is as disgraceful as a warning".
Why say "value your calamities as part of your being"?
What makes it possible for me to have calamities
Is treating myself as having a being;
Further, if I had no being,
What trouble could I have?
Hence in valuing: treat your being as the social world.
The social world may be delivered to one like that.
In caring: treat your being as the social world.
The social world can be entrusted to one like that.

14

THE
UNKNOWABLE

If you look and fail to see:
Its name is "remote".
If you listen and fail to hear:
Its name is "rarefied".
If you touch and fail to feel anything:
Its name is "subtle".
These three cannot give us warning signs.
Hence blending, we treat them as one.
Its elevation does not sparkle.
Its depth is not murky.
Stringlike, it cannot be named.
It belongs to no natural kind.
This we call "the condition of being in no condition,
A sign of no natural kind".
This we call "confused and indistinct".
Facing it you don't see its head;
Following it you don't see its rear.
If you grasp ancient ways
To deal with what's here today,
You can know their ancient origins.
This is called a way's record.

為腹不為目

15

ORIGINAL INTENT

Those in ancient times who mastered being scholars
Were mystifyingly subtle and inscrutably penetrating.
So deep they cannot be comprehended.
Generally, precisely because they cannot be comprehended,
We are forced to use constructs to imagine them.
Cautious – like crossing a stream in winter.
Ambivalent – Mmm! As if fearing those on all sides.
Exacting – Mmm! As if a guest.
Mutable – Mmm! As ice on the point of melting.
Unaffected – Mmm! As uncarved wood.
Munificent – Mmm! As a valley.
Obscure – Mmm! As muddied water
While muddy, who can gradually become clean with calmness?
While tranquil, who can gradually come to life with relentless
  activity?
Whoever secures this way
Doesn't desire filling.
Generally, precisely because unfilled,
Hence they can shroud established forms.

不知常妄作凶

16

GROUNDING AND SPONTANEITY

Go to the limit of emptiness;
Maintain a quiet steadiness and
The 10,000 natural kinds will rise together.
I use this to view these reactions:
Generally, natural kinds flourish and
Each returns to its root.
Returning to the root, call it "quietude".
This I call responding to fate.
Responding to fate, call it "fixed".
Knowing what is fixed, call it "discerning".
Not to know what is fixed is wantonly taking risks.
Know to fix on "encompassing";
"Encompassing" leads to "fair";
"Fair" leads to "kingly";
"Kingly" leads to "natural";
"Natural" leads to "ways";
"Ways" leads to "enduring";
They don't end with burial.

17

IDEAL
LEADERSHIP

The best leadership is when those below know it is present.
After that
Is one that, feeling kin to, you extol.
After that
Is one you dread.
After that
Is one you despise.
When accuracy is inadequate in it
There will be inaccuracy in it.
Reflectively – Mmm! His valuing of discourse!
Success takes form; dealings follow on one another
And the people all say "we did this ourselves".

慧智出宥大僞

18

IMPERIAL
MORALITY

When the Great Way is cast aside we have
   "humanism" and "morality".
When intuitive wisdom emerges we have
   "great artifice".
When great kinships do not blend, we have
   "filiality" and "affection".
When states and great families become
   deranged and disordered, we have
   "loyal ministers".

19

見
素
抱
樸

SOCIAL VALUES

Terminate "sageliness", junk "wisdom",
Your subjects will benefit a hundredfold.
Terminate "humanity", junk "morality",
Your subjects will respond with filiality and affection.
Terminate "artistry", junk "benefit",
There will be no thieves and robbers.
These three,
Treated as slogans are not enough.
So now consider to what they belong:
Express simplicity and embrace uncarved wood.
Lessen "self-focus" and diminish "desire".

如
嬰
兒
之
未
孩

20

UNLEARNING LEARNING

Terminate learning and have no worries.

"Uh huh" and "Huh uh"?

How much mutually separates them?

"Masterly" and "clumsy"?

What's the mutual separation between them like?

What humans fear

Cannot not be feared.

Futile – Mmm! Not focused yet.

The human crowd is radiant

Like joining in a celebration

Or a spring procession up on a terrace.

I alone am placid – Mmm! It indicates nothing to me yet.

Like an infant not yet a baby.

Languorous – Mmm!

Like having no base.
The human crowd all have a surplus
Yet I alone seem at a loss.
Mine is indeed the mind of a stupid human.
Indiscriminate – Mmm!
Ordinary humans are lustrous,
I alone am dull.
Ordinary humans are critically discerning;
I alone obfuscate.
Bland – Mmm! It's like the ocean;
Drifting – Mmm! Like I have no place to stop.
The human crowd all have means-ends
And I alone am dallying and wanton.
I alone am different from other humans,
And value nursing at mother's breast.

其精甚真

21

THE NATURE
of DAO

To encompass a permeating virtuosity
Is simply following ways.
Treating ways as a natural kind is
Simply confused! Simply superficial!
Superficial – Mmm! Confused – Mmm!
Within them, signs are present.
Confused – Mmm! Superficial – Mmm!
Within those, natural kinds are present.
Yawning – Mmm! Murky – Mmm!
Within them, germination is present.
Their germination is superlatively authentic.
Within it reliability is present.
From the past to the present
Their names don't go away.
And reads out the origin of multitudes.
With what do I know the form of the origin of multitudes?
With this.

是
以
聖
人
抱
一

22

OBJECTIVITY AND CONVENTION

"Crooked" implies "intact",
"Twisted" implies "straight",
"Vacuous" implies "filled",
"Worn out" implies "new",
"Less" implies "getting",
"Excess" implies "confounded".
Using this: sages embrace one
And treat it as the social world's paradigm.
Do not look inward, hence are discerning.
Do not affirm inward, hence are verifiable.
Do not attack inward, hence have success.
Do not empathize inward, hence survive to be elders.
In general: they simply do not contend.
Hence in the social world none can contend with them.
This is what the ancients meant by "crooked implies intact".
Could that be empty rhetoric?
Ground yourself on what is intact and return to it.

23

WALKING
TOGETHER
IN A WAY

Rare discourse is so of itself.

Inherently, a whirlwind does not last through the morning.

A sudden storm does not last through the day.

What makes these? The cosmos.

If the cosmos cannot make even these winds endure,

How much more is it the case for human windiness?

Regarding, then, those who pursue dealings in ways:

Those of ways are blended in ways.

Those of virtuosity are blended in virtuosity.

Those of loss are blended in loss.

Those who are blended in ways, ways leisurely incorporate them.

Those who are blended in virtuosity, virtuosity leisurely
    incorporates them.

Those who are blended in loss, loss leisurely incorporates them.

When reliability is inadequate in it

Unreliability emerges in it.

跨
者
不
行

24

OVERREACHING WAYS

Those who tiptoe do not stand.

Those who stride do not walk.

Those who gaze inward are not discerning.

Those who affirm inward are not verifiable.

Those who attack inward do not succeed.

Those who empathize inward do not become elders.

When these are in ways,

We say: "Excess provision; redundant practice.

Some natural kinds avoid them."

Hence those with ways, don't address them.

25

ORIGINS AND FOUNDATIONS

There is something formed as a mixture.

It emerged before the cosmos.

Solitary – Mmm! Inchoate – Mmm!

Standing alone and immutable.

Permeating all processes without limit.

We can deem it the social world's mother.

I don't know its name.

To assign an ideograph to it, we say "way".

Forced to construct a name for it, we say "great".

"Great" is to say "expansive".

"Expansive" is to say "far-reaching".

"Far-reaching" is to say "reversing".

So ways are great;

Nature (sky) is great,

Earth is great,

And kings are also great.

Within a region are four "greats".

And the king is one among them.

Humans follow patterns on earth.

Earth follows nature (sky).

Nature follows ways.

Ways follow what is so of itself.

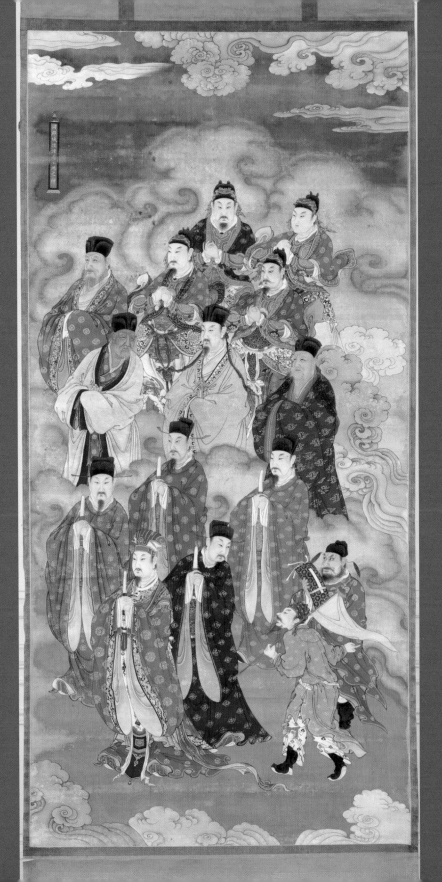

燕
處
超
然

26

HEAVY
AND LIGHT

Deem "heavy" as the root of "light",
Deem "calm" as the leader of "uproar".
Using this: sages walk all day
Without ever letting go of their heavy load,
Even while at sublime overviews,
Comfortably perched and transcendent.
What do we say, then,
When a ruler of 10,000 chariots
Takes the social world lightly compared to his own well-being?
"Light" entails losing the root.
"Uproar" entails losing the leader.

27

TRANSCENDENT MASTERY

Masterful performance ignores others' ruts and footprints.
Masterful discourse ignores flaws and blaming.
Masterful tallying doesn't need calculating devices.
Masterful closing doesn't need bars and bolts
And still can't be opened.
Masterful securing doesn't need rope or restraint
And still can't be loosed.
Using this: sages fix on mastery at saving humans.
So no human is abandoned
They fix on mastery at saving natural kinds,
So no natural kinds are abandoned.
Call this "doubled discerning".
Hence masterful humans
Are the instructors of those who are not.
Humans who are not masterful
Are material for those who are.
Were one not to value his instructor,
Not to care for his material,
Even if wise, he would be seriously misguided.
Call this the important secret.

知
其
雄
守
其
雌

28

BALANCING OPPOSITES

To know it is male
And sustain its female aspect
Is to act as the social world's ravine.
To act as the social world's ravine,
Fix on virtuosity, avoid distraction,
And return to infancy.
To know it is white
And sustain its blackness
Is to act as the social world's paradigm.
To act as the social world's paradigm,
Fix on virtuosity, avoid lapses,

And return to the absence of ultimates.

To know it is sublime

And sustain its disgrace

Is to act as the social world's valley.

To act as the social world's valley,

Constant virtuosity is sufficient

To return to uncarved wood.

If wood is split then regard it as an artefact.

Sages use it

And are regarded as officials and elders.

So great systems do not cut.

29

OVERREACHING RULERS

Desiring to take up and act on the whole social world,
I see that as impossible.
The social world is a spirited artefact.
It cannot be enacted as a construct.
Those who enact constructs for it, destroy it.
Those who grip it, lose it.
Hence, some natural kinds perform,
Some conform.
Some snort,
Some blow.
Some are strong,
Some are weak.
Some wear down,
Some collapse.
Using this: sages abandon extremes,
Abandon extravagance,
Abandon expansiveness.

善
有
果
而
己

30

ANTI-COERCION

Those who use ways to help human rulers
Do not coerce the social world with arms.
Their dealings favour reciprocity.
Where we place a division,
Thorns and briars grow.
In the wake of a great army
Inevitably lie years of calamities.
Mastery bears fruit – period!
Do not presume, with that, to coerce.
Bearing fruit, avoid pitying.
Bearing fruit, avoid domineering.
Bearing fruit, avoid pride.
Bearing fruit, treat it as out of your control.
Bearing fruit, avoid coercing.
If natural kinds are robust, they get old.
This is called "don't guide".
"Don't guide" ends quickly!

戰
勝
以
喪
禮
處
之

31

DAOIST
PACIFISM

In general, beautiful martial displays
Are inauspicious artefacts.
Natural kinds should perhaps eschew them.
Hence our ways should not include them.
If the leader is in place then we value the left.
If we use martial force then we value the right.
Martial force
Is an inauspicious artefact.
It is not a leader's artefact.
If beyond your power, you use it,
Treat detachment as the elevated attitude.
When victorious don't treat war as an art form.

And those who treat it as an art form
Make killing humans into entertainment.
If you make killing humans an entertainment,
Then you cannot work your resolve in the social world.
Auspicious dealings favour the left,
Inauspicious dealings favour the right.
The lower-rank general is on the left
And the elevated rank dwells on the right.
Its discourse, we address in funeral rituals.
Killing humans in crowds,
With bitter grief we cry over them.
Victory in war is addressed in the funeral rite.

32

SIMPLICITY, NAMES AND INSTITUTIONS

Ways fix on a nameless uncarved block.

Although small,

None in the social world can make it serve.

If fief-holding kings could sustain it,

10,000 natural kinds would treat themselves as honoured guests.

The sky and earth would intermingle and make sweet dew.

Subjects, without instruction, would put themselves in parity.

As you start to institutionalize, there are names.

As soon as there are names,

Generally, you really should know to stop.

If you know to stop, you can avoid danger.

Think of the role of ways in the social world

As like brooks and ravines flowing into rivers and oceans.

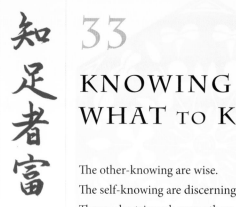

33

KNOWING WHAT TO KNOW

The other-knowing are wise.

The self-knowing are discerning.

Those who triumph over others have muscle.

Those who triumph over themselves are commanding.

Those who know what enough is are affluent.

Those who practise strenuously have resolve.

Those who don't lose their place are enduring.

Those who die and don't disappear are long-lived.

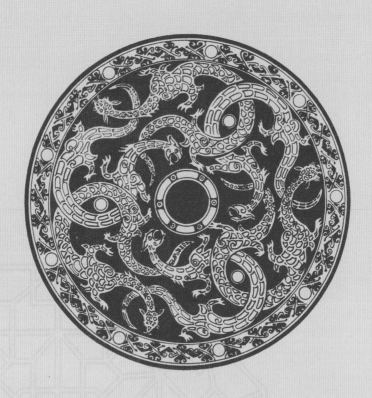

34

THE GREAT DAO

The Great Way is everywhere – Mmm!
Can it treat what is to the right as to the left?
With 10,000 natural kinds depending on it to live
It communicates nothing.
Successes taking form; it does not name it "present".
Supporting and nourishing 10,000 natural kinds;
It does not act as owner.
Fixed on lacking desire; it can be named by "small".
10,000 natural kinds return to it
And it does not act as landlord.
It can be named as "great".
Given that it never treats itself as "great",
It can, thus, complete what's great about it.

安
平
太

35

GREAT
SIGNS

Grasp great signs;
The social world moves.
If it moves and does not harm;
Tranquillity and peace are supreme.
With entertainment and feasting,
Passers-by stop as guests.
A way's coming out from the mouth . . .
Isn't it bland . . . its lack of flavour?
Look at it; there is not enough to see.
Listen to it; there is not enough to hear.
Use it; there is not enough given.

36

PRACTICAL REVERSAL

将
欲
歙
之
必
固
張
之

In desiring to contract it,
You must basically have regarded it as "expanded".
In desiring to weaken it,
You must basically have regarded it as "strong".
In desiring to dissipate it,
You must basically have regarded it as "thriving".
In desiring to take it,
You must basically have regarded it as "given".
This is called subtle discerning.
Soft and pliant win over hard and coercive.
Fish cannot leave watery depths.
The state's beneficial artefacts
Should be displayed to humans.

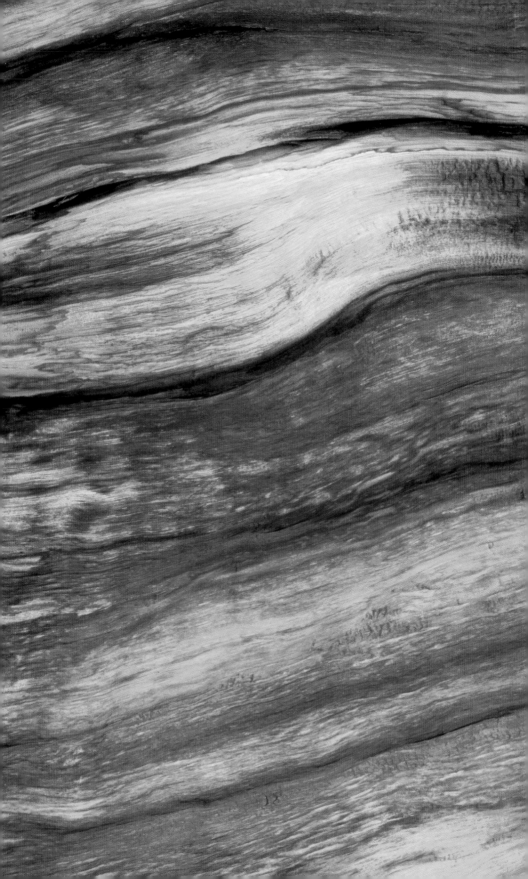

天
下
將
自
定

37

PRIMITIVE
LACK of DESIRE

Ways fix on not acting from constructs.
Yet nothing is not assigned a construct.
If fief-holding kings could sustain it,
10,000 natural kinds should self-transform.
If transforming encounters desires to construct,
I will mollify them with nameless uncarved wood.
Nameless uncarved wood is,
Generally, being about to lack desires.
Don't desire, use serenity;
The social world should stabilize itself.

38

VIRTUOSITY

Higher virtuosity does not act out "virtuousity",
For that reason it has virtuosity.
Lower virtuosity acts only on "virtuosity",
For that reason it lacks virtuosity.
Higher virtuosity lacks acting on its construct,
And lacks the construct on which it acts.
Lower virtuosity acts on that construct,
And has that construct on which to act.
Higher humanity acts humanity out,
And yet lacks acting on that construct.
Higher morality acts morality out,
And has acting on that construct.
Higher conventionality acts that out,
And answers to nothing.
It raises its arm and throws.

Hence after we lose our ways, then we rely on virtuosity!
Losing virtuosity, we then rely on humanity!
Losing humanity, then rely on morality!
Losing morality, then rely on conventions!
In general, conventionality
Is the thinning of fealty and trust,
And the forerunner of disorder.
Those who first understood that,
Tried to embellish ways,
And initiated stupidity.
For this reason, men of greater maturity
Address the thick,
And do not dwell on the thin.
Address the substance,
And do not dwell in the elaboration.
So they discard that and take up this.

故
致
數
與
無
與

39

PRACTICAL
DEPENDENCIES

Things which long ago achieved unity:

The sky achieved unity in being clear.

The earth achieved unity in serenity.

Esprit achieves unity in an ethereal aura.

Valleys achieve unity in being filled.

10,000 natural kinds achieve unity in living.

Aristocrats and kings achieve unity in acting as the social world's
   standard of "proper".

They've taken it to the extreme.

When the sky lacks the means to be clear,

We should fear splitting.

When the earth lacks the means to be stable,

We should fear spreading out.

When esprit lacks the means to be an aura,

We should fear death.

When valleys lack the means to be full,

We should fear depletion.

When 10,000 natural kinds lack the means to be alive,

We should fear extinction.

When aristocrats and kings lack the means to be valued and exalted,

We should fear their toppling.

Hence the valuable treats the discounted as its root.

The high treats the low as its foundation.

Using this: aristocrats and kings call themselves worthless lonely
orphans.

Is this not treating the discounted as the base?

It's not?!

Hence the extreme of numbering chariots is no chariots.

Do not desire the coloured veneer of jade,

Or the solid dullness of a rock.

新長龍髯過屋牆
曉雲湮處露
峰尖山中四月
如十月衣帽
惲欄冷翠霑

清湘小乘客濟圖

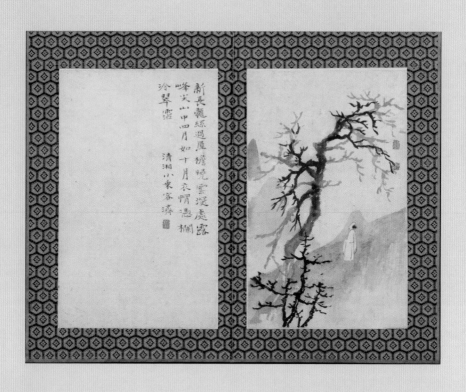

40

REVERSAL

The movement of ways is reversal.
Where there is weakness lies the use of ways.
The social world's 10,000 natural kinds arise from presence.
"Presence" arises from "absence".

不
笑
不
足
以
爲
道

41

LAUGHING
AT DAO

The "higher" scholar hears a way;
He gets all serious and practises it.
The "medium" scholar hears a way;
It's like it exists; now like it is gone!
The "lower" scholar hears a way;
He laughs hilariously.
If he did not laugh, it would do to treat it as a *way*.
Hence, as a conventional saying puts it:
"A discerning way is like a murky one.
A way to advance is like one to retreat.
A way to level is like one to rough up."
Elevated virtuosity is like a valley.
The greatest purity is like filth.
Expansive virtuosity seems insufficient.
Creating virtuosity is like stealing.
Solid authenticity is like sliminess.
The greatest square has no corners.
The greatest artefact is never formed.
The greatest note rarely sounds.
The greatest sign lacks a shape.
Ways hide the absence of names.
In general, simply because ways are
  good at contributing and succeeding.

萬
物
負
陰
而
抱
陽

42

DAO, NUMBERS, REALITY AND TEACHING

Ways generate a "one".

"One" generates "two".

"Two" generates "three".

"Three" generates 10,000 natural kinds.

10,000 natural kinds endure *yin* and embrace *yang*.

Infuse life-force and treat the result as harmonious.

What humans revile

Is simply being deemed "worthless", "lonely", or "orphaned".

Yet kings and dukes take these terms as their honorifics.

Hence partly diminishing natural kinds, they increase.

Partly increasing them, they diminish.

What humans teach,

I also teach.

Those who use coercion and stealth do not get their death.

I would treat this saying as "the father of teaching".

不言之教

43

REVERSAL:
WEAKNESS
AND WU-WEI

The most yielding in the social world
Lopes past the most firm.
That which lacks presence enters into that which lacks space.
With these examples, I know the advantage of not acting on
  constructs.
The teaching that is not put in language,
The advantages of not acting on constructs,
The social world rarely reaches this level.

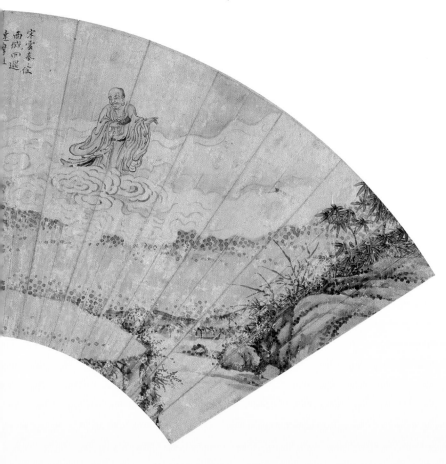

44

REAL AND SOCIAL VALUES

Take your name and your being – which is closer to you?
Your being and commodities – which counts as more?
Obtaining and losing – which is the defect?
For this reason, super care exacts great cost.
Excess storage certainly increases loss.
Knowing what is enough is not disgraceful.
Knowing where to stop avoids danger.
You can extend your life.

45

REVERSAL AT EXTREMES

Great formation is like deficiency.

Its use is not defective.

Great filling is like infusing.

Its use is not exhaustive.

Great straightforwardness is like being bent.

Great skill is like clumsiness.

Great dialectic is like shouting.

Exercise conquers a chill.

Rest conquers a fever.

"Clear" and "quiet" are treated as correct for the social world.

46

SOCIAL WAYS
AND SUFFICIENCY

When the social world has a way
We retire fast horses to fertilize fields.
When the social world lacks a way
War horses breed in the suburbs.
No transgression exceeds approving of desires.
No tragedy exceeds not knowing what is enough.
No evil exceeds desiring to obtain things.
Hence, knowing when enough is enough
Is fixing on "enough".

其
出
彌
遠
其
知
彌
少

47

KNOWING
INHERENTLY

Know the social world without stepping outside your door.

See natural ways without looking out of the window.

The farther one goes,

The less one knows.

Using this: sages do not practise and yet know.

They name things without looking.

They take form without acting on constructs.

為學日益為道日損

48

PRIMITIVISM'S
PARADOX

In acting on "study", one daily increases.
In acting on "ways", one daily decreases.
Decrease and further decrease it
Until you arrive at not acting on constructs.
No acting on constructs yet no act is not under a construct.
Fix on not using social dealings in taking up the social world.
If you accept its dealings,
It does not count as taking up the social world.

聖
人
無
常
心

49

PUZZLES
OF ERROR

Sages lack a fixed mind;

They treat the people's mind as mind.

Mastery of something, I treat as mastery of it.

Lacking mastery of something, I also treat as mastery of it.

Virtuosity in mastery!

Reliable things: I treat as reliable.

Unreliable things: I also treat as reliable.

Virtuosity in reliability!

A sage in the social world is absorbent.

Trying to enact the social world would addle his mind.

The people all focus on their eyes and ears.

Sages all treat them like children.

50

NUMEROLOGY OF LIFE AND DEATH

We emerge into life and enter into death.
Of life's associates, ten have three.
Of death's associates, ten have three.
Movements of human life towards the grounds of death
Are also ten have three.
Now, why is this?
Because they regard opulent life as "life".
In general, when we hear about mastery at preserving life:
They walk the earth without encountering rhinoceros or tiger.
They enter the army and do not bear armour or weapons.
The rhinoceros has no place to thrust its horn.
The tiger has no place to wield its claws.
Weapons have no place to insert their points.
Now, why is this?
Because they lack any grounds of death.

51

VIRTUOSITY IN DAO

Ways generate them;
Virtuosities cultivate them:
Natural kinds shape them;
And circumstances inform and complete them;
For this reason, among 10,000 natural kinds,
None fail to respect ways and value virtuosity.
This respecting of ways
And valuing of virtuosity
Is, in general, not coerced, always autonomous.
Hence ways generate them;
Virtuosities cultivate them,
Bring them to maturity, educate them,
Shade them, poison them,
Nourish them and return them.
Generating, it does not treat them as possessions.
Acting on constructs, it does not depend on them.
Living to maturity, it does not act as an "authority".
This is called "unfathomable virtuosity".

52
STORY OF THE SOCIAL WORLD

The social world has a source.

Treat it as the mother of the social world.

Since we have its mother present

We can use it to know its offspring.

Since we know its offspring

We revert to sustaining its mother.

And we're not in danger till we lack being.

Clamp its exchanges,

Close its gates,

Never striving to the end of our being.

Free its exchanges,

Complicate its dealings,

Still not rescued at the end of our being.

Seeing something small, call this "discerning".

Protecting something weak, call this "enforcing".

Use its light and

Restore its discernment.

Don't leave things to trouble your being;

Treat this as rehearsing what is fixed.

大
道
甚
夷

53

DANGERS OF
THE GREAT WAY

Let me some trivial know-how
To execute in The Great Way –
Only adding to it – this I fear!
The Great Way is supremely easy
And its subjects like short-cuts.
The palace is supremely stripped.
Fields are supremely overgrown,
Granaries supremely bare.
Clothes embroidered colourfully.
Belts have sharp swords.
Bored of drink and food.
Wealth and commodities in excess.
This is called "stealing" and "exaggeration!"
This is not a way!

吾何以知天下然哉以此

54

ABSOLUTE AND **RELATIVE**

Mastery of building does not tear down.
Mastery of embracing does not let go.
Children and grandchildren never stop sacrificing.
Groom it in one's being
And its virtuosity is in authenticity.
Groom it in one's family
And its virtuosity is in plentitude.
Groom it in one's village
And its virtuosity is in becoming elderly.
Groom it in one's state
And its virtuosity is in wealth.
Groom it in one's social world
And its virtuosity is in universality.
Hence use "self" to view the self.
"Family" to view the family.
"Village" to view the village.
"State" to view the state.
"Social world" to view the social world.
How do I know the social world's condition?
With this.

蜂
蠆
虺
蛇
不
螫

55

INNATE VIRTUOSITY

The thickness of inner virtuosity:
Consider it in a robust infant.
Bees, scorpions, serpents and snakes do not sting him;
Ferocious animals do not seize him;
Birds of prey do not strike him;
Bones weak and muscles soft; he still has a firm grasp.
Not yet knowing how male and female join; he is still
  completely hard.
The instinct has arrived!
The whole day he babbles and he does not get hoarse.
Harmonizing has arrived!
Knowing to harmonize, call it "fixed".
Knowing what is fixed, call it "discerning".
Benefiting life, call it "auspicious".
The way the mind governs life-force, call it "coercive".
If natural kinds are robust, then they get old.
Call this "not guided".
"What is not guided" ends quickly!

知
者
不
言
言
者
不
知

56

KNOWING AND NOT SAYING

Those who know how do not hold forth.
Those who hold forth do not know how.
Treat its openings as blocked,
Treat its gateways as closed.
Treat what is sharp as dull,
Treat classifications as loose.
Treat what is bright as blurred,
Treat grains of dust as together.
This is called the unfathomable togetherness.
Hence we cannot by getting something achieve intimacy with it.
Cannot by getting something be distant from it.
Cannot, by getting, benefit.
Cannot, by getting, harm.
Cannot, by getting, value.
Cannot, by getting, debase.
Hence we deem it a value of the social world.

我
無
欲
而
民
自
樸

57

NON-CORRECTING CORRECTION

Order a state by doing right.
Use shock to deploy military force.
Use no dealing to take up the social world.
How do I know these are so?
With this.
When the social world adds superstitious prohibitions,
It increases poverty of its subjects.
The more subjects have beneficial artefacts,
The more the state and society are befuddled.
The more humans become skilled and clever,
The more strange things emerge.
The more standards and commands are promulgated,
The more thieves and robbers are present.
Hence sages say:
I eschew acting on constructs and subjects transform themselves.
I incline towards calmness and subjects correct themselves.
I avoid dealings and subjects enrich themselves.
I lack desires and subjects simplify themselves.

禍
兮
福
之
所
倚

58

GOVERNMENT IN UNCERTAINTY

Its regime is torpid;
Its subjects are guileless.
Its government is critically discriminating;
Its subjects are deficient.
Tragedy – Mmm! The ground of fortuity.
Fortuity – Mmm! That which conceals tragedy.
Who knows its zenith?
It lacks any conception of "correct".
Correctness reversed we deem "strange".
Mastery reversed we deem an apparition.
Human puzzles:
Their days stubbornly endure.
Using this: sages
Square without shaping,
Investigate without punishing,
Straighten without being arbitrary,
Illuminate without dazzling.

長
生
久
視
之
道

59

CONSERVING
AND PREPARING

In ordering humans and dealing with nature, nothing
beats conserving.
In general, simply conserving
Is what we can call early readiness.
Early readiness: let us call it "emphasizing storing virtuosity".
Emphasizing storing virtuosity implies that everything is subdued.
If everything is subdued, no one knows its zenith.
If no one knows its zenith
It can have states.
The mother of having states
Can long endure.
This is called the deep root and inherent base,
A way to long-life and enduring insight.

治
大
國
若
烹
小
鮮

60

GOVERNING
LARGE STATES

Putting a large nation in order
Is like grilling a small fish.
If you manage the social world with ways
Its spirit will not become self-aware.
Even if its spirit does become self-aware,
Its awareness will not harm humanity.
Even if its awareness allows harming humanity,
Its sages will still keep humanity from harm.
In general, when the outcome is neither harms the other,
Their virtuosities interact and return to balance.

大
者
宜
為
下

61

BEHAVIOUR
OF STATES

Great states flow to the lower position.

The intercourse of the social world,

The female of the social world!

The female fixes on being still to win over the male,

Uses being still and reclining.

Hence, if great states recline for small states,

Then they absorb small states.

If small states recline for great states,

Then they take great states.

Thus some from lower use "taking",

Some are lower and still take.

Great states only desire to domesticate humans in a universal way.

Small states only desire to serve humanity.

So both get what they want.

It is fitting for great to act out being lower.

美言可以市

62

OBSCURE
WAYS

Ways are the hidden subtleties of 10,000 natural kinds.

A treasure to skilful humans.

That which unskilful humans sustain.

Aesthetic language can be marketed.

Respectful performance can enrich others.

Humans who are not good at things,

What reason is there for abandoning them?

Hence, setting up some offspring of nature

And establishing three ministers.

Then even presenting them with jade pulled by a team of horses –

Is not as good as sitting and promoting this way.

Why did the ancients so value this way?

Did they not say "seeking you get it;

If guilty use it to escape".

That's why we deem it a value of the social world.

味
無
味
大
小
多
少

63

NOT ACTING
ON CONSTRUCTS

Act on the construct "don't act on constructs".
Treat having no dealings as dealing.
Treat the absence of flavour as "flavour".
Treat the small as "great"; the few as "many";
Use your virtuosity in dealing with rancour.
Plan for the difficult while things are still easy.
Act on the great while it is still small.
Difficult dealings in the social world
Must start with something easy.
The great matters of the social world
Must start with something small.
Using this: sages, in the end, do not act great
So they can embody their greatness.
In general, frivolous assent must diminish trust.
If much is easy then much must be hard.
Using this: sages emphasize that it is hard.
So in the end it lacks hardness.

千
里
之
行
始
於
足
下

64

PLANNING
AHEAD

It is easy to grasp what is tranquil,
Easy to plan before there are any warnings,
Easy to break what is brittle,
Easy to disperse what is miniscule.
Act on it before it is present;
Put it in order before it is disordered.
Trees that fill our embrace
Emerge from small sprouts;
Nine-storey towers
Start from piles of earth.
A thousand-league walk
Starts with a footfall.
Those who act on constructs wreck things;
Those who cling lose things.

Using this: sages do not act on constructs, hence they do
  not wreck things,
They do not cling and so do not lose things.
Ordinary subjects following through in their dealing
Regularly get them nearly finished then wreck them.
If you are as careful at the end as in the beginning
Then you will not wreck deals.
So sages desire not to desire
And do not value goods difficult to obtain.
They study not-studying
And revert to what the human crowd has overlooked.
In reinforcing the autonomy of 10,000 natural kinds
They do not presume to act on constructs.

玄
德
深
矣
遠
矣

65

THEORY OF GOVERNING

Those in ancient times who were good at enacting ways
Did not use them to make subjects discerning,
But bordered on making them obtuse.
That subjects are hard to put in order,
Comes from their abundant cleverness.
Hence to use cleverness to order a state
Produces the thieves of the state.
Not to use cleverness to order a state
Is to enrich the state.
Those who know to do both enshrine models.
Fixing on knowing how to enshrine models,
Is called "unfathomable virtuosity".
Unfathomable virtuosity becomes deep! Becomes distant!
The reverse of ordinary kinds.
After it is so, comes supreme flow.

故天下莫能與之爭

66

LEADING
FROM BEHIND

The way rivers and oceans can act as kings of a hundred ravines:
Is being good at lying under them.
Hence they can act as kings of a hundred ravines.
Using this: if sages desire to elevate their subjects,
They must use language that places them lower.
If you desire to place subjects first,
You must take your being as coming after them.
Using this: sages
Residing above, their subjects deem them no burden.
Residing in front, their subjects are not harmed.
Using this: the social world leisurely advances them
  without resentment.
Since they do not contend,
None in the social world, can contend with them.

不敢為天下先

67

A DIFFERENT WAY

The entire social world calls my way "great" – as if unfamiliar.
In general, simply in being great
It is, consequently, unfamiliar.
Had it been long-familiar
It would be trivial!
I have three treasures.
I cling to and preserve them.
Call the first "charity".
Call the second "frugality".
Call the third "not presuming to act as prior to the social world".
Charitable: so one can be brave.
Frugal: so one can be magnanimous.

Not presuming to act as prior to the social world:
So one can become "elder".
Were I now to abandon charity and bravery,
To abandon frugality and liberality,
To abandon following and put myself in front –
Then already dead!
In general, charity:
Used in battle, implies victory.
Used in sustaining, implies stability.
Nature will save it.
Use charity to defend it.

善
勝
敵
者
不
與

68

SUBTLE ROLE
PERFORMANCE

Those good at playing the "scholar-knight" are not martial.
Those who are good at fighting do not rise to anger.
Those who are good at triumphing over enemies, don't
  engage them.
Those who are good at using humans treat it as beneath them.
This is called virtuosity at not contending.
This is called the power of using people.
This is called being on a par with nature
– the apex of antiquity.

禍
莫
大
於
輕
敵

69

WAR AND WINNING

There is discourse about using armies.
Not presuming to act as lord, I act as guest.
Not presuming to advance an inch, I retreat
  a foot.
This is called "practising absence of practise".
"Bearing absent arms";
"Throwing against absent enemies."
"Controlling absent armies."
No tragedy is greater than taking an
  enemy lightly.
Taking an enemy lightly risks losing
  my treasure.
Inherently, opposing armies strengthen
  each other.
Then grief is the winner.

70

UNDERSTANDING ME

吾言甚易知

My discourse is supremely easy to know.
Supremely easy to practise.
In the social world
None can either know or practise it.
Discourse originates from somewhere
And dealings have standards.
Generally, simply not knowing how
Counts as not knowing me.
If those who know me are scarce,
Then what I am is valuable.
Using this: sages
Wrap precious jade in burlap.

知不知上不知知病

71

PARADOX AND PRACTICALITY

Knowing not to know is recommended.
Not knowing to know is a defect.
In general, simply deem defects to be defects,
Then one can be non-defective.
Sages are not defective
When they deem defects "defects".
For this reason they do not act on "defect".

無
厭
其
所
生

72

ALLEGIANCE
AND RESPECT

If subjects do not fear authority
Then great authority has arrived.
Do not meddle with their dwellings.
Do not despise what they generate.
In general, if you do not despise,
Then there will not be despising.
Using this: sages
Know from "here" but do not gaze inward,
Love from "here" but value subjectively.
So they discard "that" and take up "this".

天
之
道
不
爭
而
善
勝

73

TOLERANCE AND NATURAL WAYS

Courage within presumption implies killing.
Courage within non-presumption implies living.
These pairings:
Sometimes benefit, sometimes harm.
That which nature abhors,
Who knows its cause?
Using this: sages make things even harder.
The natural way, not contending, is good at winning.
Not discussing, is good at responding.
Not calling, it comes from within.
Insensate, it is good at planning.
The natural net is all-encompassing.
Loose, it still does not lose anything.

吾得執而殺之孰敢

74

EXECUTION
AND MURDER

When subjects do not fear dying
How can one use "death" to intimidate them?
If I make subjects fixate on their fear of dying,
Then, grabbing those who deviate,
I kill them;
Who would presume to carry out the sentence?
Should we settle on having a hit man do the killing?
In general, killing in place of a professional killer
Is called "substituting a lumberjack for a master artisan".
In general, of the lumberjacks who replace master artisans
  and carve
Few manage not to injure their hands.

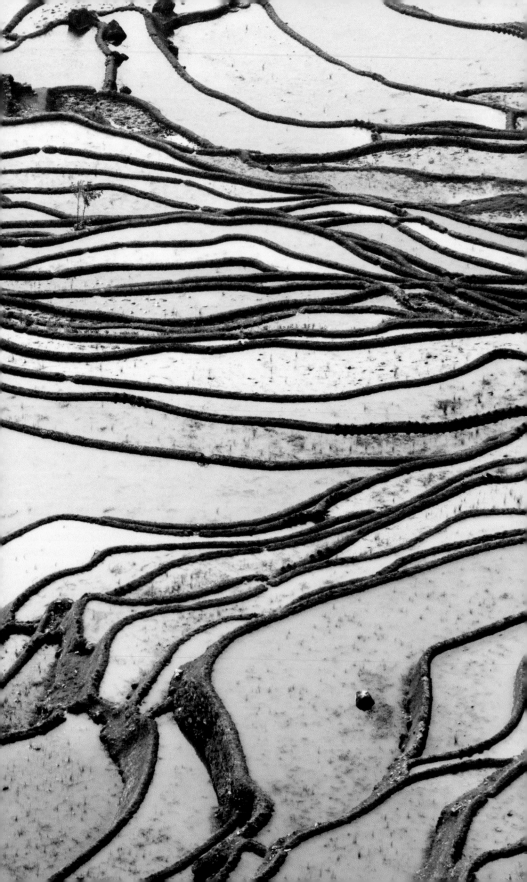

是賢於貴生

75

EATING
THE PEOPLE

Starvation among the subjects
Is because those above them feast on taxes-in-kind.
From this: they starve.
Subjects' being hard to put in order
Is because those above them act on constructs.
From this: they are hard to put in order.
Subjects take death lightly
Because those above them seek life's "thickness".
From this they take death lightly.
In general: only those who do not act on "life"
Are outstanding at valuing life.

柔
弱
者
生
之
徒

76

TOLERANCE AND FLEXIBILITY

Living humans are soft and limber.
Dead they are hard and rigid.
Living, the 10,000 grasses and wood species are soft and crisp.
Dead, they are withered and tough.
So "hard" and "rigid" accompany death.
"Soft" and "limber" accompany life.
So if armies are coercive, they do not triumph.
When wood is strong, the axe comes out.
Strength and dominance reside below.
The soft and limber belong higher.

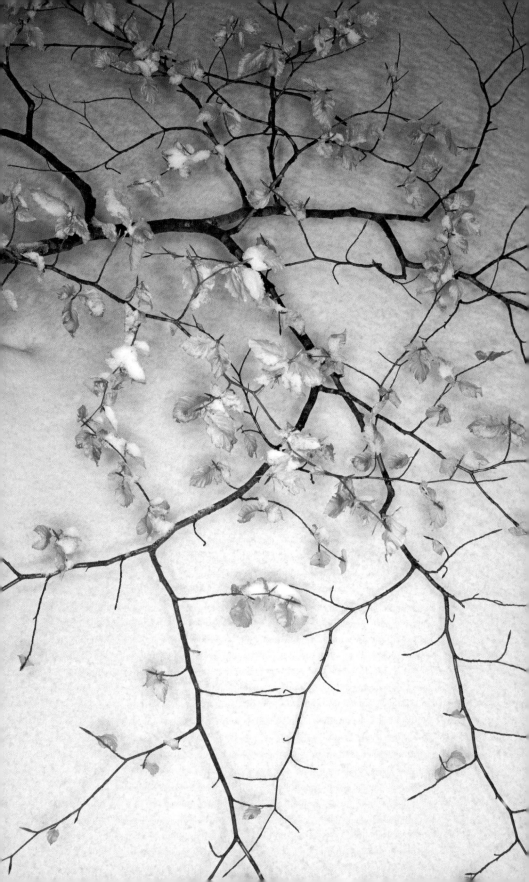

人
之
道
則
不
然

77

NATURAL AND HUMAN WAYS

Natural ways

Are they not like tensing a bow?

Pull the upper part down

And raise the lower part up.

Reduce a surplus.

Supplement what is insufficient.

Natural ways

Reduce abundance and relieve scarcity.

Human ways are not like that.

They take from those in need and give it to the well-off.

Who can take a surplus and offer it to the social world?

Only one with a way.

Using this: sages

Act out constructs but they do not rely on them.

Their success taking form, they do not notice it.

This explains their lack of desire to appear special.

弱
之
勝
強

78

REVERSAL
OF VALUES

Under the sky, nothing is softer or more yielding than water.

And yet when it attacks firm, rigid things,

None of them can win against it.

Because they lack any means to move it.

That yielding wins against force;

That the soft wins over the hard,

No one in the social world fails to understand.

No one can practise it.

So the sages say,

Accept the state's imperfections.

Correct discourse is like reversing opposites.

安
可
以
為
善

79

NATURAL WAYS
OF RECONCILING

In reconciling massive resentments,
Inevitably some rancour will be left over.
Where can that be treated as mastery?
For this reason, sages
Grasp the left side of the agreement,
Yet do not demand satisfaction from the other.
They have virtuosity in supervising agreements,
And lack virtuosity in enforcing the exhausting details.
Natural ways have no favourites.
They coordinate reliably with people who do well.

80

IDEAL PRIMITIVE STATES

小國寡民

Make states small with few subjects.
Set it up so, having implements by the tens and hundreds
They still will not use them.
Set it up so subjects, treating death as weighty,
Do not venture far.
Though they have boats and carts,
They lack reasons to ride in them.
Though they have armour and weapons,
They lack reasons to marshal them.
Set it up so subjects revert to using knotted strings.
They deem their food sweet;
Their neighbourhoods peaceful;
And their customs as entertainment.
Neighbouring communities can see each other,
Hear each other's chickens crow and dogs bark,
And their members reach old age and death
Without ever travelling between them.

善
者
不
辯
辯
者
不
善

81

WORDS AND ACTIONS

Reliable discourse is not aesthetic.
Aesthetic discourse is not reliable.
Those who are good at things, do not analyze.
Those who analyze are not good at things.
Those who know how are not comprehensive scholars.
Those who are comprehensive do not know how.
Sages don't accumulate.
Although they use things in acting for others,
They have more themselves.
Although they share with others,
They have more left over.
The ways of nature, in benefiting, do not harm.
Ways of sages: acting on constructs, do not contend.

CHAPTER COMMENTARIES

What is *dao*? Is it a thing? Can *dao* be known? Can it be spoken? What does the *Laozi* mean by "natural"? What is *wu-wei* and how can it help people? Is there something called "non-being"? Is Daoism feminist? Environmentalist? Anarchist? This section looks at each chapter of the *Laozi*, or *Tao Te Ching*, and its historical context to answer these and many other questions about the book's Daoism.

INTRODUCTION

Translation and interpretation are intimately related. The translator tries to write something in English with the same *meaning* as the Chinese text. The nature of *meaning* has puzzled philosophers since Plato and we best view it as the role an expression plays in thinking. Interpreters try to grasp what would persuade someone to think *that* and what persuading them of it would make them go on to think, say or do. Translators compromise between working at the word or sentence level; this commentary works at the level of the passage, chapter, section and whole world-view. It should be read alongside the introduction, which summarizes the philosophical context at the time the *Laozi* first emerged.

Having a commentary section and a glossary (see pages 26–35) frees a translator to shift the balance slightly toward the component concepts and structures. Otherwise, the best practice is to deliver a familiar English sentence. Translators vary renderings of underlying structures and concepts in each sentence. Emphasizing structures and concepts reveals more about how each thought links to others using those elements. The natural English sentence obscures the reasoning leading to that thought and the way it would guide them in thinking. It invites the English language reader to do both kinds of reasoning, using the translation's English structures and concepts.

It is not that a tighter word-for-word rendering is more accurate, but that each achieves different goals with different cost-benefit trade-offs. The choice made here has been to seek greater insight into the complexity of ancient Chinese thought and the commentary helps to offset any cost in readability. The translation follows the pre-Han context of the other *zi* ("masters"), but historically the text also played central roles in the superstitious Qin-Han cults, in the post-Han Neo-Daoist synthesis, in the early interactions with Buddhism, in the borrowed institutionalized monastic religion, in the Chan/Zen blending and in the later Neo-Confucian synthesis of these with the *Mencius*, and finally in a plethora of local religions revering the *Laozi*. Chinese thinkers in each context were persuaded and guided in different ways by the *Laozi*.

The commentary places each chapter in its original philosophical context and explain its role in the line of thinking then playing out (for an analysis of the concepts and structures, please see *A Daoist Theory of Chinese Thought*). This placement works more coherently in the earlier chapters. The latter portion of the second (the *De*) section (see page 232), chapters which some text scholars suspect were added after the period of the philosophers, are more receptive to the authoritarian superstitions of the Qin-Han ruler class. Readers should bear in mind all the religious contexts and reflect on how this versatile text can be read against a background of many alternative beliefs.

CHAPTER 1

DAOS, NAMES AND PUZZLES

You ask, "Where is the way?" I say: "Over there." I have *dao*-ed you to a *dao*. The way I recommended consists of other signposts, markers, or structures that you can follow correctly – or not, just as you can follow my "over there" correctly or not. If a 道 *dao* can guide or recommend something (also written 道 but used as a verb), then it's not a constant *dao*.

What is a fixed or constant *dao* – one you can't get wrong; one to which you do not need to be guided? The movements of the stars and celestial objects trace a constant or fixed *dao*. You do not ask, and I can't tell you, how to digest an apple. The process of digestion is fixed. The normal biological processes of life are naturally fixed.

The key difference between recommendable ways and fixed ones is words (名 *ming*, "names") and their counterparts – signs, markers, demonstratives and gestures. These help us to bridge the space between discourse and our situation. "There" can be used to "name" an object, property, or a way, but if I use it, you might look where I'm pointing and pick out something other than what I had in mind. You may even pick out the first signpost *over there* and still lose the way because you misread or misapply it. *Dao*s and names that guide require interpretation in each unique local situation. Guiding *dao*s cannot be fixed be-cause they rely on names (or a counterpart) that we have to interpret into concrete action in our own circumstances.

However, are there not some fixed (unambiguous) names? Are no classifications absolute or fixed – no distinctions that are basic? What about the distinction between existing and not existing? Does it depend on how one takes it? It seems like what there is – being (有 *you*, "have:exist"), which is translated here as "presence" to emphasize its context dependence – is fixed; as is its opposite, 無 *wu* ("lack-not exist"), which is translated here as "absence". "All the things there are" should be encompassed in "being" while "non-being" should *name* what lies outside the boundary of "everything".

But it turns out that these also depend on how we take them *pragmatically*. When we fix on 無 *wu* ("absence, non-existence, lack") it's because a puzzle is being addressed – something's missing. Different things are "absent" in different contexts. To fix on non-being globally is itself a mystery. Is naming "that which is outside the boundary of 有 *you* ('have-present-exist')" not naming *something*? Conversely, if we fix on *presence*, we are about to attend to what is going on, what is actually happening.

These opposite, reciprocal, concepts are interdependent – they are born together. How can that be? What distinction can we be marking with them? That puzzle is not only the gateway to many philosophical puzzles, but it would also open the way to the introduction of Buddhism into China some half a millennium later. A related puzzle in Western philosophy fuelled an analytic debate in the twentieth century.

SEE ALSO: the sections on *dao*, names, being and non-being

CHAPTER 2

LANGUAGE AND CONTRASTS

Names come in pairs, opposites. To commit yourself to one is to rule out the other. We cannot have names without these norms of permitted and forbidden use. Names guide us in partnership with our ability to make a distinction and be guided by it – toward one or away from the other. People learn each pair by learning how to make a single distinction. Social conventions govern where the correct place to make the distinction lies.

What about sages – infallible sources of guidance? Are they limited to these conventional ways of classifying, to these large, insensitive dichotomies that reflect so little of the variation within each range? The *Laozi* contrasts with the *Zhuangzi* in seeming to take seriously the idea that people can avoid such constructs – *wu-wei*. People do not need to deem things as falling into one or another of these named categories in dealing with them. Other natural creatures are born and live without making judgments about what exists or what doesn't exist.

As for the idea that sages should manage to do without these forms of social

evaluation: If you never judge something is present, that you have it, then you won't be able to judge that it is absent or lost.

SEE ALSO: concepts of the social world, good-at, natural kinds, sages, acting on constructs

CHAPTER 3

ARTIFICIAL DESIRES

Confucians were defenders of traditional morality – patterns of classifications, especially of social roles, inherited from previous generations. Both Confucians and Mohists (their rival utilitarian moralists) thought of advocating a *dao* as recommending a shared pattern of guiding distinctions for everyone in society. Everyone makes the same evaluative distinctions so that we can communicate and coordinate our behaviour, thereby maintaining *order*.

This construct-guided order is learned by following models – wise, outstanding people who guide by their example. For both Confucians and Mohists this requires that society elevates the different people each school thought of as being the best. These *elevated* individuals had privileges – things that are in short supply for most people and are deemed valuable only because of their scarcity, such as exotic foods, silk clothing, jade, gold, and so on.

One of the central insights of Laozi's work is that this valuing of rare stuff is a puzzling tendency. People end up competing for such stuff, but does it really matter that it is rare? Can that contribute more to my *natural* well being? If not, the *Laozi* suggests, it has no bearing that others also want it, particularly when the desire is socially reinforced by using such privileges to mark status, rank and success. Such things are valued only in the sense that others want them, not that they contribute to a person's survival or satisfaction. Therefore highlighting them distorts normal behaviour and channels it toward something of no natural value, fomenting competition and strife for the favoured positions. This makes the positions themselves become more political than real differences in human value. The cost of getting social organization in Confucius's way is that people lose contact with what has real *natural* value.

Laozi suggests that we keep to natural values – what we need to eat and to maintain health. We should not create systems of classification and models of mastery which stimulate people's unnatural – socially constructed – desires for empty embellishment. Only then will wise people turn their wit to real matters: rather than mastering a favoured scheme of evaluative distinctions, they will make distinctions that solve real problems and all will solve their own difficulties without social engineering or trying to identify with Confucian or Mohist "masters". This will produce a natural, spontaneous order of *real* value.

SEE ALSO: concepts of desire, concepts of the social world, mind

CHAPTER 4

REFLEXIVE *DAOS*

Ways are curious *things* – though the question arises, are they things? It seems like they are *of* things, not added *to* them. (Think of how tea is infused in water – it doesn't increase the volume.) And we use them without depleting anything.

What if we reversed the guidance that our social *daos* give us? What if we took every pair of opposites and valued the other one? This is the *Laozi*'s favourite thought experiment – the reversal of values. It seems to make sense, as if there really were something there! But where could it come from? Is it natural? Is it prior to any system of names, constructs and symbols?

CHAPTER 5

NATURE'S INDIFFERENCE

The natural world does not seem to care about the things that people care about. Mohist morality starts from an assumption that 天 *tian* ("nature:sky") has intentions – that its implicit goal is universal benefit – which should be humankind's touchstone to value. So *tian* grounds their utilitarian, goal-directed morality. Laozi expressed his scepticism at this. All things live and die – a view that is not as pessimistic as the one expressed in Buddhism, because life is not understood to consist of suffering. Life is a natural temporal process, living and dying exist in relation to each other. The same material *qi* (氣 "breath") is simultaneously living and dying. The cosmos is a process, or *dao,* of birth, death and recycling to other forms of life. It is nothing to the cosmos when a bird dies. The cosmos, even if conceived of in organic terms, doesn't care about us. A broadly organic model of cosmology blends this doctrine and that of *qi* (氣 "breath") into a natural cosmic mingling of opposites which leads to reproduction.

However, the parallel line about sages is jarring and constitutes one of the hints in the *Laozi* that sages are bad (maybe these lines refer only to Confucian-Mohist sages?). Or it could be that sages, if they really avoid acting on constructs, do not make *any* evaluations. In other words, sages are like the cosmos in just letting things take their course.

Isn't nature really empty of value? In valuing nature and natural action, are people really valuing? Or is there a paradox? Maybe people shouldn't try to talk about it and just steer a course.

SEE ALSO: the section on 天地 *tian-di,* ("sky-earth"), the cosmos, humanity, sages, and knowledge

CHAPTER 6

THE NATURAL
CREATIVE POWER

One of the reversals the *Laozi* is famous for is the reversal of conventional male-centric schemes of value. In his *Analects,* Confucius expresses traditional prejudices about females and the *status* of their social roles. The Mohists, even with their universalist tilt away from traditional roles, still didn't distance themselves much from male chauvinism. The *Laozi,* in several places, expresses admiration for the natural role, the successful strategies and creative power of the female.

The metaphorical association of fertile valleys and the fecund feminine shape suggests a more balanced appreciation of the central role of females in the production of life and of the female's relatively more successful (but less assertive) life strategies. The chapter's seeming awareness of the importance of balance and cooperation between the two offers a contrast to Aristotle's assumption that life is contributed by the male (although Daoist sexual practices could hardly be said to lack veneration for semen, which was regarded as the life essence).

The female later becomes a guiding element in the cluster of concepts associated with the 陰陽 *yin–yang* cosmology, though an oblique mention of *yin–yang* occurs only once (in Chapter 42). In later Confucian orthodoxy, female is *yin* and male is *yang.* The ancient Chinese treated cosmology on the analogy of living organisms, not the analogy of a machine or object of creative art. A broadly *organic* model of cosmology blends this doctrine and that of 氣 *qi* ("breath") into a natural cosmic mingling of opposites which leads to reproduction. Hence the absence of a Chinese appeal to a creator – being and non-being create each other. Creation is a natural process (often described in terms of penetration, mixing, and birth) and commentaries on the 易經 I Ching (Yijing) analogize sky and earth to father and mother. The entire scheme is informed by the *Laozi*'s appreciation of the inter-relation of opposites – the famous idea that at the most extreme *yang* is becoming *yin* and vice-versa. The cosmos is an endless process of blending, generating and returning.

This organic conception is implicit, but only the dependency relation of opposites is formulated in any detail in the *Laozi*. The strongest hints are in this passage. Other metaphors of creation are more mathematical or obscure (versions of chaos theory – see chapters 25, 40 and 42).

SEE ALSO: reversal

CHAPTER 7

SELF-FOCUS

Daoism survived the end of the philosophical period because the superstitious rulers were seeking formulas for long life. The resultant religious practices and alchemy were associated mainly with the *Laozi* and the cult of Huang-Lao. The *Laozi* has several hooks for this familiar human concern because any talk about a natural *dao* is going to recognize that we are looking for ways to survive – and trying to avoid those that bring quick death. However, the message is naturalistic.

The cosmos (天地 heaven and earth combined) is about as long-lived as anything. These two survive together, according to this passage, because they do not separately create themselves. They are interdependent and rely on each other (father and mother, male and female). An excessive concern for our own being is not good for a human. By turning your focus on other human beings and helping them, you help yourself. We do not need to be sages or slaves to tradition to appreciate this familiar, simple insight into morality.

Sages dedicate themselves to others, not their own status – yet, paradoxically, their well being is best achieved by not seeking it. So are they really altruistic or . . . ?

CHAPTER 8

BEING GOOD AT THINGS

Water is another element later clustered (along with female) under *yin*. It symbolizes moist, fertile, cool, taking the lower position, non-assertion, conformity, and so on. The chapter provides an example of the power of passively accepting the shape of things. It also exemplifies a natural object "finding" its way – a way that was there prior to the water's flowing into it and one that is further shaped by water's flow.

Although it is important in most elaborations of Daoism, the only explicit references to water are in this chapter and a mention in Chapter 78. It is an apt metaphor for how a *naturally* existing path results from the distribution of material in the world – the valley – and then to other natural substances *finding* and following that 道 *way*. This passage baptizes moral terms like 善 *shan* ("good-at" some *dao*) in water's example. Water does not fight things; it conforms to them and finds its way without concern about its low status or swampy home. We may be repelled, but water's "path" is a good guide to human paths – our paths tend to be nearby.

"Flow" is a good metaphor for primitivist worries about fussy Confucian morality – so filled with detailed rules of behaviour that only trained adepts could master them. The primitivists rejected social conventions and complex forms of social organization (the division of social roles). Loosely linked with Yang Zhu (see pages 21, 22), their outlook was based on the natural flow of development, which tended to be amoral.

Clearly, things can be natural for us that are not necessary, but some activities integrate naturally into our *flow* – a flow that may be a different one for each person, each *dao* and each situation. The worries about Confucianism are that its imperial, imposed morality seeks to force our behaviour into a mould in which we lose that natural flow. By contrast, natural moral compassion, reciprocity and everyday problem-solving are smoothly, spontaneously integrated into the flow of our lives.

CHAPTER 9

GETTING VERSUS ACHIEVING

The theme of reversal draws frequently on common-sense practical advice – popular sayings, lore and folk wisdom – which the text's editors have woven elegantly into the philosophical poetry. This chapter reminds us of our own lore: all good things come to an end; excessive striving for certain goals in life can defeat those very goals.

A frequent theme of this common-sense advice is that possessions can detract from one's freedom and sense of self. In effect, a person becomes hostage to their possessions – they have to lock doors, stay nearby to guard them, and so forth.

CHAPTER 10

UNFATHOMABLE VIRTUOSITIES

A controversial theme in both the *Zhuangzi* and the *Laozi* is the role of "the perfect" or "the extreme" expression of something. One may read them, religiously, as affirmations of a supernatural quality in some beings or things. More philosophical readers should see them as reminders of the practical irrelevance of the question of what a perfect person (a sage) would do. What a perfect dancer would dance isn't much help to me as I struggle with basic steps. It may *inspire* me, but it works poorly as a guide for me *now.* What God should do about disease does little to solve the immediate problem of what I should do about it, here, today.

Not only is such advice irrelevant, it is typically incomprehensible. The perfect person or God counterpart is so unlike us that we really do not understand what it is for them to be in our situation or contemplating our choices. Our ordinary practical concepts wouldn't mean the same thing to them. This chapter's theme thus dovetails with the reversal theme: a perfect example of a thing may seem to us like its opposite. As David Hume (1711–1776) argued, a God who created this world must be, at the very least, mischievous if not evil.

This ending reminds us that in following any advice based on constructs we contemplate such extremes. The chapter raises the issue with a series of rhetorical questions – which we can answer from either the religious or philosophical point of view.

CHAPTER 11

VALUING ABSENCE

We can translate the 有無 *you-wu* pair as "being" and "non-being", but we have already addressed the puzzle in thinking of them as fixed references to any absolute features of the world (see Chapter 1). In this chapter they are used in the relative sense of presence and absence (of some indicated thing), or as having or lacking some item, not as absolutes. This allows

the reader to appreciate a charming feature of Daoist thought – its appreciation of the value of absence. Besides the concrete examples in this passage, the value of absence in Chinese landscape paintings inspired by a Daoist sensibility is demonstrated by those in which space, absence (of ink, in this case), is the central feature.

In these examples, we rely on the notion of usefulness. In the *Zhuangzi* we can find parallel, but more radical, stories of the usefulness of uselessness.

CHAPTER 12

PRACTICES AND SPONTANEITY

How many colours are there? The *Laozi* was still circulating in different versions during the superstitious Han period, when the Confucian orthodoxy saw everything as being dominated by 五行 "five-element" theory. The five elements symbolized phases that succeeded each other in various orders and that interacted in various ways. For example, a period in a ruler's reign would correspond to one of five mineral categories, five directions, five sounds and five colours.

Scepticism about this model was already rife in the earlier, more philosophical classical period. This Daoist expression of scepticism illustrates another central theme: social constructs, particularly structures of fives, tend to be too coarse to serve seriously as guidance in concrete life. Our natural access to reality reveals something far more subtle, variegated and beautiful than can be captured in so simplistic a system of constructs.

The constructs are best avoided, being available to few and designed to fuel and reward competition – just like the socially "elite" activities referred to in the chapter. People should concentrate on real natural values and the natural variety immediately available to all of us. We can then envision equally enriched lives for everyone; so the sage, in governing, attends to essential needs – food and not fashion.

CHAPTER 13

SOCIAL APPROVAL AND VALUE

In the *Zhuangzi's* history of Daoist thought, an account of a philosopher named 宋鈃 Song Xing precedes its discussion of the *Laozi* and the *Zhuangzi*.

Song Xing originated an important Daoist distinction between social status and real (ethical) value, for which the authoritarian Confucian Xunzi denounced him. The *Laozi* here takes up Song Xing's insight – favour is disgraceful. However, the *Laozi* develops it in an interesting way that expands the insight. Status (like rarity) is an artificial desire that contributes to competition and therefore to social strife. So the Confucian recipe for social order – the designation of a hierarchy of roles for positions of leadership (and privilege) –

carries the seeds of its own failure, namely strife and disorder.

This is because the individual who receives "favour" gets it from someone above him in terms of social status. So, in valuing it, the recipient must implicitly acknowledge his lower status, and hence value, in comparison with the one conferring the "favour" on him. And if we value the favour, it implies we regard others who did not receive the favour as diminished. Thus, we should regard favours as disgraceful because they imply inequality of worth.

We should, by contrast, value hardship, calamities and struggle – they are the evidence that we are active, *real* beings. One couldn't be in trouble unless one were a human being.

If we really valued ourselves as participants in a social world and thought of our identity as having been constituted in that social world, then we would treat it as something integral to our being. Someone who has that attitude toward the social world can be trusted as a leader. In contrast, those, like the Confucians and Mohists, who treat themselves as social engineers, capable of taking the social world as an object and constructing it according to their *dao*, are dangerous. The message of the chapter is that, only if you identify with and care for yourself as integral with the social world, can the rest of us trust you.

CHAPTER 14

THE UNKNOWABLE

Dao is not an ordinary object or a natural kind. We get guidance from apprehending the configuration of things – for example, a road is an arrangement of cobblestones and vegetation. We only grasp *dao* in what we can see, hear or touch, but we assume, even when we can't access the guidance, that it stretches "stringlike" through things as well as in our past and present practices and natural history.

Like the *dao* that we cannot see in things that are too remote in space or time, we can't directly access the *dao* in the history of our practices. We learn a practice as it exists now, but we have to extract something that fits our situation now in order to get guidance from it. *Dao* is somehow enshrined in historical practice the way it is in physical arrangements. *Dao* is something we have to extract from nature by understanding a social practice's origin, purpose and role all through its history. It seems that in using that *dao* to solve *this* problem we have mystically pulled something from ancient practice.

If we extract guidance from history we use it to grasp what counts as following that *dao*. That makes a performance, or "walking", constitute a correct execution of prior practice. Who is in a position to judge if we have done "the same thing" in these different circumstances? (Think about how US Supreme Court Justices will disagree about what decision counts as "following precedent".)

This chapter offers us an elegant and pragmatic formula. Find something that works in the present context; if it does, treat that as having found what was *correctly* implicit in past practice. We can catch on and continue in *our context* with success – as we judge it from the perspective of that *dao*. To do this is to grasp the import of the past practices, as knowing what counts as *following* them. The real basis of the correct *dao* is that it works in our present situation to solve *this* problem. Then we say we know what an ancient *dao* records.

CHAPTER 15

ORIGINAL INTENT

A tempting, but mistaken, way to think of what is enshrined in past practice is to project an idealized portrait of the ancients to whom we attribute the invention of the particular practice.

This is what Confucians do with their idealized sage kings (and what conservative US Supreme Court Justices do when they appeal to the "Founding Fathers"). We attribute to them almost supernatural cognitive and predictive abilities and then imagine to ourselves how these "ideal intellects" would judge and act. Copying this imagined act is correctly following what is enshrined in the traditional practice.

However, when we draw these portraits, do we wonder on what they based *their* ability to decide what to do – and subsequently to transmit to us? By hypothesis, a practice or *dao* had not *then* been invented, unless we postulate an endless series of still earlier generations of sage kings. So, in a situation of even less information than we have, how did they figure out what everyone should do for all time?

Because we imagine these people with no prejudices and commitments, we seek to use them to give more legitimate status to our conventional behaviours. The concepts we use to describe the ancient ideal are the social constructs arising from those very conventional practices. All we achieve by this fantasy is to shroud the conventionality of our guiding attitudes and give them special authority as "interpretations" by ideal sages. How someone with no established practice would interpret our established practice is irrelevant to how we should interpret and perform them in our context. Imagining how supernatural idealized founders would act is little help in figuring out what I should do here and now.

CHAPTER 16

GROUNDING AND SPONTANEITY

Some credit Daoism with an environmental sensitivity; others with an openness to science. Expressions, especially of the primitivist attitude (see Chapter 9), hint at both

– but they are vague hints. If we could quiet our practical drives, desires and attitudes and just contemplate the organic unity and complexity of the ecosystem, then we could see how all the natural kinds interact and how the system maintains its balance. We see flourishing, dying and regenerating in a quiet, natural equilibrium that seems never to be disrupted. This is natural *constancy*, what is *fixed*. If we can discern what is fixed and distinguish it from what we can change, then we can avoid unwise risks. We know that what is fixed is the compensating balance of the whole system, as if there were some kind of natural fairness and equality. Appreciating this naturally qualifies one for political leadership. This leadership style, with its continuity with the natural processes, can endure even after their own reign ends and they are buried.

CHAPTER 17

IDEAL LEADERSHIP

Chinese social–political theories place less emphasis on punishment and law than Western theories. Their idea of leadership is typically more organic – more like opinion-leaders, natural chiefs and fathers than law-makers. Confucians and Mohists both envisioned a spontaneous acceptance of someone outstandingly wise as a leader, albeit with their warring conceptions of what counted as wise. The *Laozi* in Chapter 17 similarly contemplates a leader who seems barely to be there. This suggests there is no need for the social world to have leadership from a single person other than as a figurehead. An ideal social dynamic, like the natural one, should stabilize and flow without direction from above.

Mohists had imagined a scheme in which practical judgments about right and wrong ways to go about things would be systematically "reported up" the hierarchy to the natural leader who would make the final selection, then pass the resulting *daos* back down the hierarchy so everyone judges things the same (supposedly best) way.

This would be only second best to a Daoist ruler who would let people go on discovering and sharing, informally, their ways of doing things. Still worse than that would be the kind of rulers China actually had – those who imposed norms of behaviour by a system of punishments meted out by local magistrates; a system that was unresponsive to local know-how. That result will be worse when the norms are so absurd and unprincipled that you have contempt for the leader who promotes them, whether efficaciously or not.

Best simply to let people find what succeeds, talk about it, trade ideas and spontaneously work things out for themselves.

CHAPTER 18

IMPERIAL MORALITY

When humanity became reflective and tried to substitute a scheme of judgment for natural know-how, it began to debate ideals of virtue (like Confucian 仁 *ren*, "humanity") and schemes of morality (like Mohist utilitarian 義 *yi,* "morality"). Both represent a decline from natural spontaneity.

However, with these constructs of virtue and morality we discovered that we lack a categorical natural standard of right and wrong. Self-styled moral sages then asserted special, intuitive access to morality – one which gave their views on these things precedence over those who disagreed with them. Natural wisdom, which we all have, is practical know-how, the ability to successfully solve our everyday problems. Public celebration of a special, intuitive, inexplicable and unjustified sage's intuition about morality undermined this natural know-how. When such intuitive moralities are accepted, pretend-prophets, hucksters and other con-men will be happy to take advantage of public credulity to gain status and privilege.

Confucian morality is characterized most famously by a moral demand to love our parents, especially our domineering, autocratic fathers and older siblings (particularly our elder brothers, in rough order of their age). Daoists think such a morality is sign of something's having gone wrong in natural parent-child and brother-sister relations. Love and respect for one's parents and older siblings should be a natural process, not the demands of an imperial morality. When we see 孝 *xiao* ("filial piety") emerge, we know we are well into serious decline.

In the fragmented disorder produced by this progressive decline from naturalness, we get political structures, coercion, states and powerful families who use hoodlums and gangsters to intimidate the rest of us – and all, of course, are totally beholden to a privileged few at the top, the 忠臣 or "loyal ministers".

When things have disintegrated so badly, it's time to contemplate again the benefits of natural anarchy – not chaos, but spontaneous social cooperation in local contexts. Give up on moral empire.

CHAPTER 19

SOCIAL VALUES

The mechanism for the decline was the introduction of constructs to guide our behaviour. These constructs have no natural, practical content, and they exist only in socially structured guides imposed on the social world by Confucian or Mohist social engineers. The way back to natural association – spontaneous, autonomous morality – is to reject these terms of domination and to cease acting on their constructs.

Stop talking about sages and their special wisdom so we can get back to figuring out how to improve our crops (the word for "benefit" refers most concretely to harvesting). Get back to natural, spontaneous love of family and neighbours, without moral manipulation or haranguing; get rid of aesthetic "sophistication" and the valuing of rare objects.

We will reach a state symbolized by the famous "uncarved block" – natural wood before the social distinctions and constructs are applied. In this state, people will lack artificial desires for competitive status roles fostered by Confucian and Mohist morality. The state of uncarved wood is the state of freedom, spontaneity and natural autonomy, governed only by face-to-face conversational relations with others.

The chapters are editorial conventions and, at this point, many interpreters take the first line of Chapter 20 to be the conclusion of this chapter – it works very well. However, either way, we should read chapters 19 and 20 sequentially.

SEE ALSO: "benefit–harm"

CHAPTER 20

UNLEARNING LEARNING

Really, to recover our natural spontaneity, we have to remove all the distinctions that come from group behaviour. We should remember (and remind each other) that these distinctions don't have a real practical basis but instead play roles in our social lives. We absorb these in our own attitudes – fear what others fear and smile at what others smile at.

However, at our beginning we didn't naturally have this pattern of attitudes. We could be in a ceremonial crowd and not appreciate that it is festive and is supposed to portend something good. We stay uncommitted and open to all possibilities because we can't be sure how things may turn out. The authors liken this to new-born infants, before they have absorbed the social constructs of "yes" and "no" or the meaning of a smile.

We learn patterns of behaviour from the moment we are born, but how do we know to attend to social activity at the very first? We do not have a sense of any place to return to – like a home. Others may think we are dull, unable to participate with them in their clever debates, using words. But we quickly catch on to what matters to us now – babbling and charming our mother – we survive in the natural way, nursing from the breast.

CHAPTER 21

THE NATURE OF *DAO*

One of the issues dividing Confucians and Mohists was the moral focus. Confucians emphasized 德 *de* ("virtuosity") and the Mohists focused on *dao*. Confucians want us to learn character from officials, who model correct attitudes and character. Mozi argued that constructing a public discourse to guide behaviour correctly would do more to shape correct attitudes and character. However, later Mohists began to worry about how to incorporate a requirement that knowledge of names should fit with reality. Daoists agree that *dao*s are more basic and that *de* is only our natural ability to follow *dao*s – an ability we acquire from following them as well as from teach-

ing. The social *dao*s we follow, though, are continuous with natural *dao*. We find structures in the real world that invite us to follow them and that have a high probability of success.

Thinking of *dao* as a natural kind, a thing or a force, is confusing. Things are composed of 氣 *qi* ("breath:life-force"). *Dao*s are not themselves composed of *qi*, but structures (openings) produced by the natural arrangement of things composed of *qi* around – like valleys and mountain passes. The distribution itself is a product of natural *dao*, like erosion and evolution. The distribution and arrangement of 氣 *qi* ("life-force") generates natural kinds, the things for which our social languages have names. The social world's conventional discourse contains signs with evolving patterns of use. The changes result from users' seeking and following natural ways then integrating them into the evolving discourse. How we recognize and classify things (structures of *qi*) is partly a product of natural possibility and of evolving social *dao* (the changing conventions of use) of our names.

The natural opening and invitations to us are the most "authentic" level of *dao*s. Each kind for which we have names has its own internal guides to its reliable reproduction and germination. Our paths of possibility intersect with the paths of other living things. This is the most accurate basis for naming – the reliable forms that persist over time. Our social discourse *dao*s should reflect the natural *dao*'s evolution – its history from past to present – so names can guide us in solving problems consistently over time. If we rely on the authentic natural level in interpreting the multitude of phenomena, we will understand where things come from. Knowledge is not rooted in dictation from authorities, but in direct contact with "this" – the situations in which humans use demonstrative pronouns and successfully solve their own real-time problems.

CHAPTER 22

OBJECTIVITY AND CONVENTION

These opposites imply each other; to have a concept of one requires us to know to rule some things out. So the concepts have a real use, grounded in distinctions in the world. The later Mohists and the *Zhuangzi* (especially the reputedly authentic "Inner" chapters) referred to this role of words as 辯 *bian* ("distinction dispute"). This is a term the *Laozi* employs, though rarely and in the later chapters where it reflects only *bian*'s use to refer to the disputes that are centered on how the parties deploy these distinctions – especially evaluative ones.

Plausible candidates for the "one" ("sages embrace one") are these distinctions, which create each pair of opposite terms; or it may be the field in which the two opposites draw the distinction or division; or it may be the sages' favoured side of each opposition, the one by which they seek to guide the social world. Sages do not focus only on their own use, but think of how everyone would best deploy each distinction. The sage's judgments should have public criteria and a wide range of application in space and time.

The sage is not asserting personal authority. He is taking a variety of points of view and blending them. In taking guidance from the totality of the social world's usage, the sage is not disagreeing or guiding that use, so he does not invite disagreement or conflict. Thus society stays intact with itself and with nature. That is what we should do.

CHAPTER 23

WALKING TOGETHER IN A WAY

If we accept the *Laozi*'s advice about the natural, autonomous evolution of our social discourse *dao*s, we will discover that while unity is possible, change is inevitable. Very little of what is in language is fixed by nature, so it will change quickly. Zhuangzi also played on the analogy of 言 "discourse" and 風 "wind". The Confucians wanted to restore the social world's guiding discourse back to forms dictated by sage kings and then stabilize those patterns of use. The Mohists wanted a social discourse developed – one that would have popular participation, but be organized and directed by an authority structure that would pass final judgment, unify in the social world judgments on that decision which should stand as 常 *chang* ("constant–reliable–fixed"). Mozi's justification for this was a remotely natural one: such an arrangement naturally produces greater utility because it conforms to nature, which plays the role of normative authority.

Daoists challenge this hope for a constant discourse and envision a more autonomous organic and evolutionary role for discourse – like a "windstorm that does not last the morning". We can walk together in a way, or in patterns of virtuosity in executing a way, but we will begin to notice the loss of reliability and fidelity in our *dao*s of interaction with each other and with nature around us. We notice this as unreliability or inaccuracy in our shared discourse – so discourse naturally evolves too. Your way of acting and my way of acting become our way of acting – ways are easily aggregated and embrace us together. The world "plays" our discourse *dao*s out of us and then "plays back" its natural counterpart. We can hear the harmony or the dissonance in the resulting duet and adjust our execution spontaneously. Daoists are simply less impressed with either role for authority; they regard *dao*s themselves as the source of normative authority, neither 天 *tian* ("nature, heaven, sky") nor 聖 "sages".

CHAPTER 24

OVERREACHING WAYS

We may, again, be tempted to step outside ourselves, to try to gain a transcendent perspective beyond the ongoing interaction between our social discourse *dao*s and the natural results of our 行 "behaviour", something above the evolving natural *dao* of possibilities. This is overreaching. We can only judge from where we are and adapt spontaneously. We should not try (as the moralists do) to deliberately engineer our ways. We do not treat them as objects of our manipulation but as spontaneously evolving tools that adapt as we use them.

CHAPTER 25

ORIGINS AND FOUNDATIONS

This chapter's more elaborated account of a natural cosmology invites the analogy of origination from chaos. It characterizes the mixture of 氣 *qi* ("breath:life-force") as chaotic, and creation as the churning generating natural patterns of homeostasis – natural kinds of things. The main difference from the account implicit elsewhere is the idea of a pure chaos in the beginning. All explanation starts from *qi*.

Much of traditional cosmology is symbolized in folk-theories of Chinese characters. The cosmos (the sum of sky and earth) forms a top and bottom frame for the social world. In the original Confucian picture, the king is the link that ensures continuity and connection – a relationship reflected in the symbol for king 王.

What produces this structure from the energy-stuff? The structure is not itself a *thing*, but the result of the distribution of thing-stuff – *qi*. We can refer to it – the way [chaos came out], but is it really there prior to the distribution outcome? The *Laozi* refuses to call "*dao*" a name and calls it instead a 字 *zi* ("character"). (Written Chinese does not use an alphabet but elegant and efficient graphs or characters for whole words or concepts.) This reminds us how the concept of name is tied to that of natural kind, attribute or social matter. If we must name the natural structural feature of paths, we can say they are "extensive, everywhere, through all times and reversible" (we can *walk* them either way).

So, in addition to the elements symbolized in the character for "king" we have a *dao* of that whole evolving system. All the elements obtain guidance out of different parts of the structure. We read things going on here on earth to guide us; earth cycles according to the seasons marked in the sky; the sky's constant movement follows *dao*; and even *dao* is not a separate standard – it is just each thing spontaneously following the paths of possibility in the natural structure. *Dao* does not command but flows, emerges from the autonomous doings of each thing in the cosmos.

The word *ziran* is usually translated as "natural", which we also use to translate 天 *tian* ("nature:sky") and the Confucian notion of 性 *xing* ("nature"). The subtle difference can be appreciated by noticing that the compound *ziran* consists of a reciprocity marker (自 sometimes translated as "self", but without the implications of the technical Western notion of an active substance in which a person's properties inhere) that

also carries some of the sense of "from". *Ran* is anything we can say of some topic – what is "so" of it; thus the compound is "so of/from itself". It is often translated as "spontaneous", but the compound suggests a kind of autonomy – not the control of an object like "mother nature". However, the autonomy is not of a self, but it does imply an absence of outside authority. A related compound in modern Chinese is *ziyou* – from "the self" or "freedom". Daoism is China's philosophy of freedom.

CHAPTER 26

HEAVY AND LIGHT

The puzzles in this chapter are the implied priority of distinctions, because normally they are balanced. Here, the argument for one being the more important is a kind of punning moral for political leaders: if you make light of the social world's affairs, the uproar will bring about lack of a "leader". The general theme seems to be understated economy and lack of self-assertion. Other chapters rehearse this theme of treating the social world as light, relative to one's own interests.

CHAPTER 27

TRANSCENDENT MASTERY

Perfect practical mastery is nothing like the kind of mastery real people can achieve, but we can think of it as a pointer to a direction of greater mastery. The more we achieve mastery, the less we are dependent on the ordinary tools we use in learning – the 轍 跡 "roots and footprints" of others. The *Zhuangzi* frequently suggests this is a kind of achievement in which a component of skill becomes second nature, so our brains call that whole sub-routine in the process of executing some larger plan.

The subject matter of which sages should achieve mastery should be a universal one – saving all humans (in the manner of a *boddhisattva*) . . . or even all things (another hint at an ecology theme). Sages should move beyond distinctions in their concern, hence beyond human versus non-human; however, as they do that, they move away from relevance to our most pressing concerns.

If we confine mastery to the practical level among humans, then we can see the point of teaching and learning. If we try to go beyond that and imagine situations without their human context, we will find ourselves getting confused.

CHAPTER 28

BALANCING OPPOSITES

This chapter returns to emphasizing balance and interchange between opposites. We should appreciate that with each distinction and set of opposites, there is a guiding value. In the Han era, Confucians in particular

came to be associated with the primacy of 楊 *yang* (the male, higher position, activity, and so on). They portrayed Daoists as emphasizing the opposite values. However, the Daoist point is to see the role of both, not to treat one as primary. In knowing one, we should preserve the other.

A total focus on acquiring skills recalls when we were infants. Children are naturally engaged in age-appropriate learning, starting with the control of their limbs, to walking and talking. Nothing distracts them from this natural acquisition of virtuosity. The model for all understanding should be the way children come to recognize the light-dark distinction. They do not rely on social constructs. In learning to talk children are acquiring social constructs, such as terms for moral status. However, they do not discard things because of low status. Being concerned exclusively with achieving virtuosity at local *daos*, as the infant is, is like returning to the state of 樸 natural simplicity – like uncarved wood, before it has been "cut" and marked by guiding terms. The social cutting and the statuses, like "sage" and "elder", are social artifacts, institutional roles, embodiments of traditional practices. Sages who exercise these institutions become authorities. However, the greatest institution is one that does not cut (does not rely on names, roles, status, or rank). The greatest institutions are egalitarian.

CHAPTER 29

OVERREACHING RULERS

The conception to avoid is one in which we imagine ourselves constructing the norms of judging the whole social world. Logically we can't do it since we have to use norms of judging in deciding what to construct for the rest of us. What do we use for that? If we use the existing norms, we tilt toward Confucian traditionalism; if we use Mohist utilitarian norms, we undermine the natural, evolved moral structure that we use in producing (and judging) utility. Either way, to try to guide the social world is to undermine and harm it.

Things happen. Some conform and some transgress. Each part of an ongoing, evolving society deals with things in different ways and the outcome determines the direction of the social world and its ways of judging. Don't try to leverage yourself out of this process. Don't aim for superlative, supernatural, transcendent points of access. You are a part of it and guided by it even as you seek to reform it.

CHAPTER 30

ANTI-COERCION

Military people have natural *daos* but the *Laozi* urges that they not be used to help rulers impose either a Confucian or Mohist (or any other) scheme of judging people. Anti-military pacifism is a widespread theme in Confucian and Mohist literature, though Mohists accuse Confucians of serving too willingly as tools of the ruler. (Besides conducting funerals, the main line of work for a Confucian was as a state official, whereas Mohists were craftsmen, defensive engineers, scientists, semanticists, and knights-errant. But the line of thought leading to Laozi then to Zhuangzi in the *Zhuangzi* history of thought suggests that all the thinkers were motivated by a desire for impartiality, for more inclusive points of view, and for the absence of strife and war. The thinkers of the classical period all reacted against the pattern of conflict that gave the period its name – the Warring States. The observations in this chapter, about the devastation of life caused by the passage of an army, are classics of Chinese pacifist literature.

Of course, people want to master *daos* because to successfully pursue them 有果 "bears fruit" for them, but it should stop there. The use of coercion to enforce and rigidify our mastery over others cannot be justified. People should focus on having practical effects, not trying to control their use and ownership – the ownership of our mastery is not its purpose. We should want only to do things right – to be successful.

In the end, any success is local and situational. Whatever is robust is also in the process of expending its youth and getting old. Knowing this invites passive stoicism – that is, not being guided at all and accepting everything. Paradoxically, any attempt not to guide our efforts is a way of guiding our efforts. The advice not to give advice 不道 cannot last. The *Zhuangzi* replaces this stoic quietism with ordinary engagement tempered mainly by curiosity and tolerance, both motivated by modest scepticism.

CHAPTER 31
DAOIST PACIFISM

One hardly needs to comment on the powerful anti-war symbolism here. Military force and war are bad omens; avoiding them is a rare and valuable achievement. When we have no choice but war, do not valorize and glorify it. Do not write plays and books celebrating those who excel at killing. Do not make killing a form of entertainment if you want to contribute to the order of the social world.

The aesthetic of war is most fittingly expressed in the language of funerals. Mistakes and miscalculations in policy may sometimes require it, but the powerful expression of grief at a funeral reminds everyone in attendance of the masses of people whose lives are ruined and wasted by warfare.

China's rulers, appreciating that the military was the source of the chief threats to their power, had established a pattern of taking control with military force then either quickly disbanding their army or sending it to the outer boundaries of the empire. (It is probably an irrelevant coincidence that the text's "left" and "right" roughly correspond to our political spectrum.) Having

high-ranked generals in an administration tended to lead to fatal military coups. These arguments were notably developed by China's Legalists – another group of thinkers who, like Daoists, were named, by Han historians, after their dominant concept. Interestingly, the most prolific Legalist writer also (probably) wrote the first commentaries on the *Laozi*. The shared focus of Daoism and Legalism was dispassionate neutrality in political/social theory. However, the Legalists shared neither Daoism's pacifism nor its commitment to tolerance and autonomy.

CHAPTER 32
SIMPLICITY, NAMES AND INSTITUTIONS

The uncarved block metaphor neatly knits the key elements of the *Laozi*'s theory of names and 無為 *wu-wei*: society, artifacts, institutions and desires. This chapter illustrates the frequent ambiguous grammatical contexts that plague translators. Ancient Chinese writing relies on word order to signal grammatical structure, but it lacked inflections and punctuation; subject terms were optional, even in declarative sentences. This can make it hard for readers to determine whether a sentence should be read with imperative or declarative force. A reader of the original can choose to treat 樸 *pu* ("uncarved wood") as the subject of the second sentence or the last word in the first – a head noun modified by 無名

"nameless" forming the object of its main verb. This translation adopts the second option, hence "nameless uncarved block", because it sacrifices no content, adds detail and emphasizes the metaphorical role of uncarved wood initiated in Chapter 28. It also makes the first sentence more relevant to the chapter's theme.

"Carving" in the metaphor symbolizes the social distinctions governing the use of names. Society, in cultivating a pattern of distinctions, constructs two words associated with it with which we guide our 欲 desires and hence our 為 wei ("deeming action"). The socialized distinctions create both constructs, which in turn create artificial desires and complicate our relations to natural dao. Uncarved wood is the metaphor for the state prior to this socialization, which works by the contrast of a natural object (wood) and the utensil or implement produced by carving it. Implements are natural substances (wood) given a social use (a goblet, for example) by our practices, by our social dao. Constituted of natural stuff they exist relative to both social and natural daos. Carving metaphorically represents the distinctions names introduce. Carving or naming creates artifacts, things whose identity derives from humans' institutions and social practices (ranks, emblems, fame and so forth). Practices are rooted in names and language. The "social carving" generates an enhanced world of new potential objects of desire, aspiration and, consequently, competition and strife.

The primitivist theme in the Laozi is a powerful expression of faith in that natural dao – faith that absent institutional carving, natural daos, would lead us to solutions and to natural relations of harmonious co-existence and cooperation. Our schemes of cooperation may be local, temporary and matched to our circumstances and personality. If we can accept that we do naturally find ways to work together and rest content with that, we will not engage in the ambitious attempt to spread our mechanisms to encompass ever more people and territory, or to make it endure beyond its natural life. Chapter 80 valorizes this village ideal of simplicity, which stands in contrast with the aspiration for empire and unifying "all under heaven". These become attempts to leverage our spontaneous social daos into detached, free-floating and self-sustaining structures independent of the course of nature – that's foolish and dangerous.

A social dao is like a stream or a brook. It is something that emerges naturally from the flow of water and may be flooded out, disappear, or even be overgrown as the course of nature changes. When people start building dams and trying to control the river (especially the Yellow River) we embark on an endless and ever more complicated struggle with nature – one that in the end we will lose. (One major contrast between the Laozi and the Zhuangzi is the degree of attachment to this primitivism. The Zhuangzi is more likely to accept that the primitivist utopia is a matter of degree – it still involves some socialization – and that the tendency of successful social schemes to preserve themselves and spread is as natural as is their emergence.)

CHAPTER 33

KNOWING WHAT TO KNOW

The noun 人 *ren* ("human") is often used almost like a pronoun – others in contrast to the self. It helps for translation that our use of "others" contextually implies "other humans". While knowledge of both self and others is treated as positive, the knowledge of self, self-control and a realistic appreciation of our own real needs is more basic. (Remember, the self being controlled is not the metaphysical, Western "self" – a mind or body "substance" that is the stuff to which all our attributes are attached. Chinese 自 *zi* ["self"] is a reciprocal to the local contextualized perspective, the "here-now-this" perspective from which we must grasp and apply natural distinctions and choose natural paths. It is not a metaphysical substance intimately related to the abstract, particular, stuff of soul.)

Chapter 14 referred to Song Xing, one of whose slogans was "the essential desires are few and simple". The most direct route to knowing when we have enough is not to value the artifacts created by social norms, particularly those linked to status, role and mere scarcity. They have value only in the artificially stimulated desire of others. Keep focused on real needs and you can feel comfortable. In general, stay grounded, practise your skills, keep track of where you are and where you came from. If you stay close to this core, you are more secure.

CHAPTER 34

THE GREAT *DAO*

Passages such as Chapter 34 tempt some modern interpreters to draw parallels with modern cosmology (although there may be a cosmic bias toward left-handedness in neutrinos). However, the ancient Chinese antecedent of the idea discussed here is a philosopher named Shen Dao, who is cited as an early inspiration in both Daoist and Legalist accounts of the progress of [their] thought. In the Daoist account, Shen Dao used the notion of "Great *Dao*" to refer to the actual history of everything, past to future. Thus he drew the conclusion that we simply *will* follow the Great *Dao* and that it makes neither conceptual nor normative judgments. The crucial consequence of his conception is that it is practically and normatively irrelevant. However, Shen Dao treated the Great *Dao* as a norm – a reason for a kind of stoicism: relax, stop trying to learn anything.

Most interpreters assume the concept entails fatalism. (Technically, it is only *logical* determinism – true by virtue of the meaning of the concept. All the Great Dao implies is that what will be *will be*.) The *Zhuangzi* history characterizes Shen Dao's slogans as principles for the dead, not for the behaviour of the living – and that Shen

Dao's *dao* is not a *dao*; for example, it does not guide. However, the concept does hint at a point of reference that lacks normative relevance. *The Laozi*, especially in its primitivist mood, draws explicitly on Shen Dao's notion of the Great *Dao* three times (and perhaps implicitly elsewhere). Laozi's anti-knowledge theme echoes Shen Dao's "abandon knowledge; discard self" – but with the *Laozi's* freedom motivation. Great *Dao* was mentioned in Chapter 18, where its technical sense did not seem important – the point could have been made by talking about the natural (*tian*) *dao*. In Chapter 34 it seems almost a direct invocation of Shen Dao's conception of the space–time totality; that is the sum of "all that is the case". Ludwig Wittgenstein uses that formula to define "the world", which is one reason to avoid that English term for translating other Chinese concepts such as the cosmos (sky-earth) and the social world (the under-sky). Wittgenstein's "world" corresponds to Shen Dao's space–time "Great *Dao*".

The core feature that Shen Dao and Laozi attribute to the Great *Dao* is that it is irrelevant to the evaluation of concepts, norms of use and judgments. They conclude that Great *Dao* (like the cosmos) makes no judgments. They agree that Great *Dao* (like the cosmos) makes no judgments. But as the *Zhuangzi* history reminds us, that practical conclusion does not follow from Shen Dao's conception. In fact, so boldly stated, his slogan contradicts itself – it is the knowledge that we should abandon knowledge. If I follow that slogan, then I violate it.

Zhuangzi takes a more correct stance in his famous image of the "music of nature". Human judgments are part of the chorus of nature. Nature does not endorse or reject any of its particular voices, does not privilege any of the actually existing schemes of judgment over others; not because it judges them as equal, but because it doesn't make *judgments*. Even if schemes of concepts endure and spread via evolution, the cosmos is not thereby judging them right; it's merely bringing about that they survive and dominate the population.

CHAPTER 35

GREAT SIGNS

Are some social constructs, signs and words naturally better than others? Some may make a social world more flexible than others; some may make social systems more or less destructive of other forms of life; some are more peaceful and satisfying to their adherents; some attract those from the outside to join in – but naturally better? The words do not taste any better.

People can attend to nature as closely as they want, and it will not tell them if theirs is a better system of norms of discourse. That information is available only pragmatically. We solve a problem, remove a frustration, achieve a satisfaction. But we have to rely on some norms of "solution" and "satisfaction" to get pragmatic answers. There is no pivot from which we can leverage a cosmic answer.

CHAPTER 36

PRACTICAL
REVERSAL

This chapter develops a central dynamic of the *Laozi*: the contrast theory of language. It connects it to the distinctions and paired contrasts to desires associated with one of the constructs. A desire to X requires a prior judgment – that of not-X. However, the concluding fragments seem like disconnected non-sequiturs. The first and last are more common themes in the *Laozi* but their metaphorical connection with fish in water is obscure.

CHAPTER 37

PRIMITIVE LACK
OF DESIRE

The first line of this chapter seems to overstate a recognition that our schemes of social constructs are optional – that they could be otherwise. Or it overstates the sound point of Chapter 34 – constant *daos* do not endorse any existing scheme over others. However, this expression, in acknowledging the paradox that 無為 *wu-wei* is itself a construct, hints as more subtly recognizing the *Zhuangzi* point – that natural *dao* governs all such schemes. Conventional terms ground schemes of interactions that are not inherently rational, but persist because of the benefits of shared communication and cooperation. These benefits outweigh the benefit of changing to an alternative way of coordinating our judgments. When a ruler enacts such an ideal, he allows things to change. The primitivist moral still seems overstated. It suggests passive acceptance –mollify with the nameless, uncarved block, which reminds us to discount desires grounded in social constructs. We serenely observe how the social world evolves and self-corrects. Philosophers call this "quietism".

CHAPTER 38

VIRTUOSITY

The text was traditionally divided into two sections, often referred to as the *Dao* and *De* sections. Plausibly, the traditional title, 道德經 *Dao De Jing* (*Tao Te Ching*), derives from this fact. Each section takes its name from the subject of its opening sentence – *dao* from Chapter 1 and *de* from Chapter 38. Most scholars regard the second section as the less philosophical and more practical/political of the two. It is rather less subtle in stating its primitivism, less cognizant of paradoxes in its anti-language message and more inclined to overstatement.

In the Legalist-tinged Mawangdui silk manuscripts, the second section came first. However, a later archaeological recovery of a still earlier selection from the text confirmed the traditional order.

The theme of this chapter, despite its subject, does not suggest that 德 *de* ("virtuosity") is prior to *dao*. It is consistent with the traditional analysis of *de* as an internalized ability to execute a *dao* – the way a *dao* is programmed in a person (or thing, including the hard-wiring that allows us to take up training). The best *de* is not focused on trying to get *de* but only in trying to follow the relevant *dao* correctly. Confucians, by contrast, did focus on virtue (particularly their moral virtue of 仁 *ren,* "humanity") as if for its own sake. A post-Buddhist Confucian, Wang Yang Ming, criticized that traditional focus, as *Laozi* does here. Trying to get virtuosity for its own sake is a form of self-absorption which undermines real moral achievement. It paralyzes the actor who can only achieve 德 *de* ("virtuosity") practice in executing *dao*, and that exercise is only helping when we are focusing on doing it right. Talking about virtuosity is not merely a distraction, but an invitation to substituting pride in the display of moral quality for real moral behaviour. Our focus should only be on execution – doing it right. Real virtuosos do not think of themselves as aiming at virtuosity, but on giving the best interpretation of this piece here, now, in this venue, for this audience. Those who engage in displaying virtuosity for its own sake usually don't give the best performances and thus fail to be virtuosos.

A related point can be made for the favourite virtue of ancient China's moralists, *humanity*. Humane people act on their humanity (the feeling which is named), but do not treat their own humanity or the name and status in Confucianism as the reason

for such action. The behaviour arises from the cultivated disposition. Moral people act on morality and do so because it is moral. They act directly on the concept and construct the concept for that purpose. Conventional actors act on conventions but for these we can give no deeper answer or reason. They are arbitrary products of history. It's like throwing with no target and then drawing a bull's-eye around the impact point. Conventionalists achieve skill at arbitrary performance, so they undermine more important forms of commitment.

The theme develops an argument from Chapter 18. We emphasize virtuosity when we lose access to a *dao* itself. We emphasize humanity when we lack access to virtuosity; emphasize morality when we have lost humanity; and conventionality when we cease to appreciate what is moral. When we get to conventionality, we know there's nothing worthy of real trust in it and that we're just staving off disorder. Those who appreciate this and start gilding and elaborating conventional *dao*s merely make people more credulous. Sound, mature judgment would tell us to focus on full, *thick*, virtues, not the thin judgments of conventional gentlemen with their showy marks of traditional status. Choose here-now-this and reject distant standards of action.

SEE ALSO: 德 *de* ("virtuosity")

CHAPTER 39

PRACTICAL DEPENDENCIES

Integrated harmonies – homeostasis – is achieved in different ways in different realms. The sky is unitary when it is clear of dust, earth is unitary when it has stable balancing cycles, awareness or sapience when integrated in our psyche and personality, living things and water-collecting valleys are made whole by playing their role in a flourishing ecosystem. Similarly, achieving social harmony is done with a standard of what is "unifying" for the king. When the sky is overcast, we should expect thunder and lightning; when earth gets unstable, we should worry about landslips and earthquakes; when sapience is not integrated in our psyche, we should anticipate death; when the valley dries out and the ecosystem falls out of balance, we should fear extinction. And when kings do not inspire our sense of higher value, they are likely to be overthrown.

Things must be in balance and that means ongoing dependence on the traditionally lesser pair in all conventional oppositions. We recognize this in modest speech even among aristocrats – we should not get attached to meaningless baubles, nor even to ordinary rocks.

CHAPTER 40

REVERSAL

This short chapter sums up several earlier themes rooted in the contrast theory of language. The later Mohists gave 反 *fan* ("reversal") its technical meaning. They say ox and non-ox are *fan* and that in disputes over *fan* one side is rights. Our social *dao*s consist of constructs, contextual values, but a natural (and prescient) guide can value the opposites of these constructs. Good advice frequently tells us to reverse conventional wisdom.

The preference for the negative side of paired values leads to a familiar Laoist conclusion in this chapter. Given the context, it is best treated as a familiar claim about words. We could treat these two lines as a Daoist *Genesis*. All thing-kinds emerge from 有 *you* ("have:presence:being") and 有 arises from 無 non-being (a passage that might interest modern cosmologists). A different, but possibly related, creation story follows in Chapter 42.

CHAPTER 41

LAUGHING AT *DAO*

Which scholar has the right attitude? Given that the *Laozi* typically values the lower and the "higher" takes an obviously conventional attitude, we might argue the lower has it correct. If you can 聞 "hear" a *dao* it's probably not a constant one and can be reversed. I enjoy thinking of the three attitudes as a dialectical cycle. We can imagine successive arguments for taking each scholar's point of view. The theme of moderation might favour the middle scholar. As we've seen, daos do seem to have a strange kind of reality – not as things, yet in some sense real and natural; as empty space between things, inviting passages. So they seem a mix of being and non-being. The middle scholar sees something real – seeing them as now present where there is absence.

The chapter leaves the decision (on the right attitude) to the reader. The summing up may be either a comment about daos that you *can hear* or it may be a dismissive claim about the *lower* scholar (here taking the traditional value attached to the "higher"/"lower" distinction).

The remainder of the chapter continues the linked themes of the contrast theory of language: reversal of values (ways we can achieve something by aiming for its opposite), and the irrelevance of extremes or ideal types. The final theme dominates – the extreme of one construct is so like its opposite that it cannot be a practical guide to either. Elevated virtue is depressed like a valley. The ideal square cannot be a standard because it has no corners. It pursues this theme by using terms to identify *daos* first and then to identify 德 *de* ("virtuosities"), followed by a range of other illustrative opposites. The point of each depends on which theme we think dominates: a) the practical irrelevance of extremes, or b) the reversal theme – aiming for the opposite.

The series begins and ends with the central topic – *dao*s. What should we conclude about laughing at them and their flexibility? The central link is the way that *dao*s are found in real, unique situations marked not by stable names but direct engagement with pronouns like "this", "here", "now". Names and constructs must start from and resolve back into such direct demonstratives. This ties them to the specific point of view in which a *dao* could possibly guide us.

CHAPTER 42

DAO, NUMBERS, REALITY AND TEACHING

We can also treat this passage as either about concepts (numbers) or about reality – natural kinds. It works best if we take it together with Chapter 40, add Wang Bi's assumption that 道 *dao* is 無 *wu* ("lack-absence"), then, if we further treat *wu* as a zero we can read number theory. If *zero* is a number, then we have *one* number, this gives us two numbers, zero and one. These two and one (the number two) make three, and so on all the way to 10,000 (and beyond). However, there is little evidence of such abstract theory in other contemporary thinkers. And its result can be only endless numbers, not 10,000 natural kinds.

We find related passages in the *Zhuangzi* – the most relevant is Zhuangzi's observation that in saying there is something, we have *one thing* and *the saying/referring to it*, so there are *two* and that process gives us 10,000 things. He concludes, we cannot coherently say "all is one" without being committed to many, then observes that the same conclusion follows even if we start with 無 *wu* ("lack-absence"). Another obscure passage traces beginnings of beginnings of beginnings. . . Most likely the core insight of this passage is that numbers, like contrasts, are part of our discourse *dao*. In committing to one of them, we commit to many, so they have something in common with the other constructs for groups of five 五行, 陰陽 *yin-yang*, and 物 *wu* ("thing-kinds"). This passage is the only one that directly invokes this *yin-yang* and 氣 *qi* ("life-force") cosmology.

However, there is again an abrupt shift of theme and a fragment that reworks themes found elsewhere (chapters 6 and 39). Reversing the values in a *dao*, promoting the opposite of what it promotes, is illustrated in practical terms by sound insights from farming: sometimes by culling a herd or thinning a bush, it thrives and increases. The chapter ends on a slightly threatening example. The violent and coercive do not get the kind of death they want – their *favoured* death. It calls that lonely fragment "the father of teaching". This is another example of what tempts text theorists to suggest that the *Laozi*'s chapters are merely unrelated fragments cobbled together by the editors.

CHAPTER 43

REVERSAL: WEAKNESS AND *WU-WEI*

The chapter starts with a familiar claim about the reversal of opposites, which glides into an image that reminds us of the *Zhuangzi*'s famous example of virtuosity in a *dao*. The *Zhuangzi* tells the story of a butcher, 丁 Ding, who claims that he never has to sharpen his knife. The knife-edge has no thickness and emptiness lies at the joint between the bones. So Ding's knife-edge never touches. Ding acquired his skill, he recounts, by learning constructs – he saw the ox as parts, like a chart. After nineteen years of practise, carving is now something Ding does simply by being in the moment. Ding does not even see the individual oxen, but open ways for his infinitesimal knife-edge to effortlessly flow through. It is as if the *dao* pulls Ding's blade through the ox.

The *Zhuangzi* frequently observes that while someone like the butcher can teach his craft to others, he cannot convey the knack of adapting a teaching in words and constructs to real-time smooth flow of action in the specific, always changing, local contexts. Either students catch on after some teaching and carry on in other situations, or they do not. No modelling or instructions can fully close this gap between instruction and performance, nothing that can guarantee teaching will lead to correct practice. That's a sense in which no guiding *dao* can be constant – guaranteed to work.

The kind of ability that can realize the benefit of acting without constructs is rare in the social world.

CHAPTER 44

REAL AND SOCIAL VALUES

The opening questions in this chapter alert us to the artificiality and unimportance of the values generated by social practices and linguistic constructs. 名 *Ming* ("names") does double duty in Chinese as rank, fame, or status – here in contrast to one's well-being, which then contrasts to material goods. The more real, more natural, values are obvious. Artificial values give us too much to care about, so even a normally positive value such as caring loses its guiding role when it becomes extreme. If we seek superlative values, caring so much that we try to satisfy all of everyone's so-cially induced desires, then caring is likely to incur a great cost in real quality of life. The more we multiply value, the more we will lose. The bigger the economic bubbles of socially magnified value, the more violently they will burst.

So it is important to know to stop maxi-mizing when you have enough. That is how to avoid danger and endure.

CHAPTER 45

REVERSAL AT EXTREMES

This series of reversal examples illus-trates again how idealized or supernatural standards of behaviour are irrelevant and incoherent for us. The extreme of each value appears to us as being guided by its opposite value.

The *Zhuangzi* uses the concept of "for-mation" to refer to the outcome of arbitrary circumstance in our lives, the things that actually shape our bodies and our action-attitudes – our 心 *xin* ("heart-mind"). The distinction between filling and infusing mirrors an analysis from the Mohist dialect-ticians of how words combine. The "Inner" chapters section of the *Zhuangzi* also uses their concept, 辯 *bian* ("dialectic:distinc-tion"), more analytically.

Although the theory seems to be pre-supposed in the *Laozi*'s theory of opposites, this is one of only two chapters in the *Laozi* that explicitly use the term. A focus on lin-guistic distinctions is a central theme in the analytic philosophy of this period. It in-forms most thinkers' understanding of the moral and philosophical disputes concern-ing what is right and wrong.

The *Laozi* deals with the disputes but pointedly avoids relying on the analytic terms. Maybe the group of Zhuangzi's stu-dents who started to compose deliberately ignored or erased this focus (along with the related analytic use of 是非 *shi-fei* ["this-not this"]) to make the text seem ancient.

Its reemergence here may indicate a later generation of editors.

Another manifestation of their possible revisionism is also found in the way later students and editors reworked the history of influences leading to the *Zhuangzi in order* to minimize the role of Zhuangzi's interactions with Hui Shi. Hui Shi was Zhuangzi's dialectician friend, debate partner and quite possibly his teacher. One of the commonly cited contrasts between the two Daoist texts is this evidence of Zhuangzi's interaction with Chinese dialecticians.

Paradoxically, the arguments between Zhuangzi and Hui Shi were mostly about Hui Shi's tendency to jump prematurely to the kind of anti-language position found in the *Laozi*. Attending more carefully to analysis than did Hui Shi, Zhuangzi saw more clearly the incoherence of drawing extreme primitivist conclusions – and his followers, in writing Hui Shi out of Zhuangzi's intellectual biography, repeat Hui Shi's anti-language error. The text's examples obliquely illustrate the usefulness of the opposite values, but then end tilting toward primitivism.

CHAPTER 46

SOCIAL WAYS AND SUFFICIENCY

When the social world has a *dao* it should be a way of dealing that does not inspire chaos and war. When it lacks such a *dao*

war is a natural consequence. (It is not clear if the condition is having a single *dao* or a coherent network of pacifying *daos*.) However, whatever *dao* it has should not encourage, invite or approve desires, particularly not the artificial desires for social versus natural goods or excite and educate consuming activities. Either creating desires for rare objects or disvaluing desires for easily accessible natural things invites discontent. Cultivating a taste for "fine" wines makes us sense deprivation when we have "adequate" wine. A social *dao* should teach people how to achieve contentment with their life. That's the *dao* that keeps war horses away.

The conclusion illustrates the pattern of characterizing a *dao* by its main guiding concept, in this case "enough". Others include "well-being" for selfish *daos*, "benefit" for utilitarian *daos*, and so on.

CHAPTER 47

KNOWING INHERENTLY

The marks of later and less reflective editing are becoming more evident in this second scroll, the *De* section. Increasingly it seems the "sage" interprets the passage in a way that misses its point. This is a credulous departure from the sceptical and critical tone about alleged "sages" and their conventional "knowledge" in the more philosophical chapters (the section constituted by chapters 1–37).

Knowing what to do is grounded on what is near the specific context. The more general and far-reaching our guiding theory, the less it gives us the guiding knowledge that we need. Even sages had to start from where they were. They were not practising comprehensive *dao*s inherited from other sages. They had to start naming things demonstratively, seeing something for the first time and figuring out how to deal with it in its real-time context before they could assign it to a category.

CHAPTER 48

PRIMITIVISM'S
PARADOX

Here is another example of a *dao* (guide) being identified with its central concept – study and ways. Acting on the former is being scholarly; acting on the latter is being practical. Confucians emphasize study of the past and the steady accumulation of cultural guidance. However, the pursuit of a more natural *dao* would mean forgetting undoing past learning until we reach a state of behaviour unguided by constructs. That does not mean our behaviour can not fit under constructs, merely not be construct guided. We would guide action by immediate awareness of the needs of the situation and follow our practice as a guide to how we use words. We find the constancies in the social world through direct response to other humans, not responses constrained by their social status or role. A person will

still have "dealings", but without presupposing a prior structure other that what is practical. We are not taking responsibility for the social world if we take its current norm structure for granted.

CHAPTER 49

PUZZLES OF ERROR

Confucian orthodoxy treats the minds of sages as the standard of right – an "ideal aristocracy" conception of ethics. Mohists represent a modified view: their sages' minds consist of the constant natural principle of general utility. However, for Mohists, the sages merely know the correct standard, they don't posit it. Here, the *Laozi* envisions a radical reconception – the standard for a sage is the people's intentional posits.

The sage judges by the shared norms of the social world and uses words as the whole community does, including the terms of normative or practical evaluation (good-at, beautiful, and so on). However, he approves even of flawed performances. This could be because he sees the good in all of them or that he takes the actual outcome of all performance to constitute the reigning practice. To be perfectly responsive to the whole, social practice is virtuosity in the use of practical terms of evaluation – this is virtuosity in these values.

The sage does this both with terms of moral evaluation (善 *shan,* "good-at") and of faithful promising and description (信 *xin,* "trust"). So the sage is in the social world and absorbs its norms, while at the same time tracking their evolution in practice. Were he to try to guide or direct this process, to act on a construct as the Mohists and Confucians do, this would disrupt his mind. The people of the society all act in their context, guided by their eyes and ears; sages respond as loving parents to their children: they always see the best in them, accept them for what they are, and let them build meaning in context around their concrete lives.

SEE ALSO: humanity, humans, others, the people, subjects

CHAPTER 50

NUMEROLOGY OF LIFE AND DEATH

十有三 ("Ten have three") is neither "thirteen" nor "three-tenths". Interpretations have split over how to understand this expression, but it probably does not matter to the philosophical issue here. The theme is what causes, signals and accompanies long life and death? People go from life to death because they come to value the richness of life. Who can stop the march from birth to death? Only the fantasy character with no vulnerabilities; no place for a rhinoceros to gore him or a tiger to claw him – it's not that this character has armour, but that he (luckily) does not encounter either. This is to lack the possibility of death.

Should we conclude from this that Daoism provides a guide to eternal life? That is doubtful. Ideal invulnerability is meaningless and irrelevant to us.

CHAPTER 51

VIRTUOSITY IN *DAO*

Things come about in natural ways. Each also has its internal adaptive ways to get energy, nourishment and growth. Each natural kind's way of growing yields a characteristic shape, which each organism's circumstances and environment modifies to form its completed specimen. This notion of completion applies not only to our bodies but to our attitudes and commitments which, as Zhuangzi reminds us, grow along with the body.

Natural kinds following this natural way of development are drawn to the inviting structures open to them in their context – to "ways". Natural kinds seek these ways, select among those found, then behave as guided by them. All natural kinds value especially their skills in doing this. This attraction is not coerced; it comes autonomously from within each specimen – from its nature or 自 *zi* ("self") 然 *ran* ("so").

Ways and virtuosities are integral to all stages of a thing's growth, its education, and eventually in completing its natural cycle (reproduction and decline) and returning to where it started. Ways themselves do not have any intentionality; *they* do not operate on constructs such as ownership, authority or even existence. *Dao*, unlike God, does not rest and say "it is good". Dao's virtuosity at dealing with everything needs, and has, no deeper explanation.

CHAPTER 52

STORY OF THE SOCIAL WORLD

A social world also has a beginning – as if it were born. Its story, like that of natural creatures, is also a complex of its way of coming-to-be, its character, techniques and circumstances. We draw on past practice to know its future directions (or guidance). We extract from the practice how to go on here and now. Then, in appreciating how to take it forward, we "learn" and express fidelity to its origins 母 *mu* ("mother"). Our "correct" (successful as judged by us) appreciation of the norms enshrined in past practices, sustains them. And thus we (and our society) endure – until, inevitably, we don't. If we close our practices off from internal exchange and from outer influences, then we neither attempt nor achieve anything. If we open social *dao*s up to internal and external stimulus we change them, but even this still cannot prevent their natural decline and eventual disappearance.

To appreciate fine detail is to be "discerning" (明 *ming*) and to protect weakness is to show strength. We use the insights gained from past practice but still rely on our contextual discerning of subtle applications to help us avoid trouble. This constitutes trying to practise what is constant and fixed in social *dao*s.

CHAPTER 53

DANGERS OF THE GREAT WAY

We understand the 大 *da* ("great") 道 *dao* ("guide") as the course of actual cosmic history – all that ever was or will be the case. Appreciating the normative irrelevance of this concept, we will see that what we must avoid is treating it as we do guiding *dao*s – choosing to follow or interpret it. There is nothing to acting on it, so people use it to shirk responsibility. They disengage and regard the consequences as fate.

Then things go horribly wrong in the social world. It falls out of harmony with the natural way. Still all the time, we count as following the Great *Dao*. People starve, wars break out and it's still the Great *Dao*. Doing whatever we actually *do* do is not *following* guidance. The Great *Dao* does not guide; it is not a *dao*.

CHAPTER 54

ABSOLUTE AND RELATIVE

This chapter starts with more examples of how ideal types are irrelevant to our actual situations. We deal with real contexts in which the opposites commingle and perfection is unrealistic. We think of our constructs as ideal types, but we can cultivate them in different ways in progressively expanding realms – for example, through individual prudence, in the family, the state and the social world. In each of these realms, the associated virtuosity (the internal guide to finding that *dao*, interpreting it and evaluating the outcome) has a different character. Maximizing individual prudence is an authentic value; embracing more, we address success for a family, then for a village, and so on, until we talk of success for the social world – 天 *tian* ("nature:sky") 下 *xia* ("below") – where we rely on a natural universal value.

However, in each of these realms we judge success from that realm's standpoint; each has its own standard of success. So how do I judge the condition of the entire social world? From this, what is going on right here and now!

CHAPTER 55

INNATE VIRTUOSITY

As we acquire and groom 德 *de* ("virtuosity"), we should not forget our rich, natural, innate virtuosity. The passage here reflects, somewhat fancifully, on the implicit know-how found in the human infant. It manages, in its context, to avoid local dangers. It has the skills and behaviours that accomplish this by conditioning and manipulating others: its cuteness, its capacity to structure the interests of its parents and to attract concern from strangers are examples of a baby's virtuosities. An infant has natural reflexes that launch it on a massive programme of learning – at first just to control its body,

but then to talk so it can join in with others. The order of that learning programme is guided from inside – its internal *dao* or its natural *de* ("virtuosity"). A baby is not strong enough to walk or to hold things, but spontaneously it knows to exercise its limbs in ways that help to make subsequent learning possible. The male infant, knowing nothing of the male–female distinction and procreation, already gets strong erections; knows nothing about languages, but loves to make eye contact and exchange babble and sounds.

A natural "hard-wired" *dao* governs this natural infant behaviour, which prepares infants to acquire social practices, skills and other virtuosities. This hard-wired guidance is constant, fixed or natural. Our ability to 和 *he* ("harmonize") is what makes us able to catch on and continue social ways – music, rituals, language. This natural understanding, which contributes to life, is a good omen because all *dao* relies on and draws on it. And when the natural process yields a normatively autonomous 心 *xin* ("heart-mind"), a guiding faculty that can take control of the physical stuff of the body and surroundings, it becomes a force in nature. Its 氣 *qi* ("breath") harmonizes and recruits *qi* around us for our actions.

This robust natural integration of the *qi* in natural kinds with the surrounding *qi* in our environment enables the organism to reach an old age – at which point the forces weken and decline. One can't escape the final return and blending of our *qi* with that around us, but that does not mean no *dao* guides the organism while constituted by *qi*. If we did not have the natural guiding *dao*, we would not last long.

CHAPTER 56

KNOWING AND NOT SAYING

Some insights can help in understanding the primitivist theme in Laoism, in particular advising us to abandon language, names, distinctions, and action guided by social constructs. The difficulty of forgetting may be offset by reversing opposites. The three-character structure (*X* its –*X* 同 其塵 "together its dust" = treat the specks of dust as forming one item) of lines three to eight instruct us to "treat as *X*" what is "not *X*" in it. The point of this exercise is to help us see that acquiring know-how does not require any particular scheme of concepts and doctrines. Kids who know how to ride bicycles do not need to know the physics of gyroscopes; a physicist might know the mathematics perfectly but be unable to ride a bike. Coaches need not be good players.

This theme develops central insights from the *Zhuangzi* which rhapsodizes frequently on how know-how can surpass teaching, language, and distinctions and treats this as important insights into higher levels of skill. We learn routines to link together in higher-level guidance. We identify the parts of a guide in different ways as our mastery advances. At each level,

we cease taking the subroutines as given and we forget how we first broke them down. As we advance, the earlier levels are converted to subconscious processing. But no teaching can guarantee it – we do it spontaneously when we reach a skill level *for us*. We eventually reach a level where the whole skill becomes second-nature – when it blends so continuously with innate responses that we cease to think of any steps.

To illustrate, consider how a child learns to walk. The child at first focuses intently on shifting its weight, placing its feet, and so on. Quickly, however, those concerns become automatic subroutines. We think only "walk to the door" not "shift your weight to your left foot and move your right forward". The same happens as we learn to speak our mother tongue, and even when we learn reading and writing. We soon cease sounding words out. Skills become automatic as we achieve higher virtuosity. Like chess masters, we may come to evaluate chess arrangements with something that resembles aesthetic appreciation more than calculation (which is why chess masters can beat computers).

The more religious alternative is to treat the primitivist ideal as a kind of anti-intellectual reaction against all cultural practices, particularly those in which language lies at the core. Thus, the advice is to revert to the state prior to any learning. The error of primitivism is turning this natural process accompanying greater mastery into extreme, unrealistic advice – as if we could achieve mastery by deliberately forgetting what we have learned.

Someone who appreciates the core of Zhuangzi's insight could read these passages as observing merely that good players need not be good coaches and vice versa. We can understand the slogans as versions of a coach's advice, such as "stop thinking so much". We soundly interpret this as advice not to break the flow of action by mentally rehearsing learned slogans as we might in cramming for a test. But this advice is appropriate only after we have achieved a high level of skilled flow through practice, so it becomes possible to detach from conscious processing. We need not assume coaches are telling us to ignore everything they taught us. Alternately, we should treat it as advice to keep practising until the flow *spontaneously* becomes second nature. Someone who tells us to relax and "let our skis guide us down the hill" would not (or shouldn't) give that advice to a beginner. But at that point, they are not really teaching so much as saying: "You're ready; trust yourself."

However, a coach is not really *teaching* when they tell us we're at that phase in our learning – but saying only that can be important, for example to our confidence in performance. If we do not have the knack, then the instruction makes no sense to us. We can partially grasp it – it may be advice to relax, but we cannot practise it like a skill. It's not part of a learnable technique. It does not change the prior training, or even reinforce it. It's just a judgment that we're at the point where the teacher can't give us

anything more by way of a teaching. "Catch on and continue" is what we do when we successfully *take* the training; it is not part of the training. "Getting it" does not benefit or harm our skill level. If we read this chapter in the light of this *Zhuangzi* conception, then we regard the social value as our catching on, our being able to continue. We do not look for the social value in the words used to tell us we're ready.

CHAPTER 57

NON-CORRECTING CORRECTION

One notable absence from the *Zhuangzi* is a political philosophy. Zhuangzi's attitude was to distance himself from the dangers of political involvement during the struggles of the Warring States period (453–221BC). The *Laozi* seems geared to remedy this gap but its political advice is primitivism. The incoherence of this as the political moral of Zhuangzi's pluralistic relativism particularly starts to show up in this more political section of the *Laozi*. Many of its chapters touch on themes directed as advice or guidance to rulers – it risks formulating a rival conception of governing with the same assumptions as Confucians and Mohists. So it fits poorly with the meta-ethical detachment that underlies Zhuangzi's criticism of Confucians and Mohists. Furthermore, it fits uncomfortably with its more critical analysis of Confucian and Mohist assumptions about the role of politics. Implicitly it adopts the moralists' guiding assumptions – that we need a social hierarchy in which political leadership engineers and inculcates a unified social *dao* in its subjects.

This primitivist advice then takes the paradox of reversal simply to say that leadership should inculcate the opposite values. This political turn is what we read as a tilt toward libertarian, *laissez-faire* government permitting or inviting anarchy. The chapter starts with more conventional-sounding advice for governing – do what is correct, and in conquering use 奇 *qi* ("strange") stealth and surprise. Then the chapter reverts to type and says do not try to "take up" the social world, if through circumstances one is already in charge then do not engage in any social dealings 無事 *wu-shi* ("lack-dealings"). How can we follow all the slogans? Simply by finding oneself in the situation of being a ruler.

This chapter then recovers by elaborating the more Daoist idea that the normal goals of leaders (namely, engineering and instilling moral *dao*s) are self-defeating ones. Giving people *dao*s that restrict them will impoverish them more; giving people utilitarian tools opens up complexities with which our established practices cannot deal; building up clever intelligence will generate more previously unknown outcomes; and, the most often cited example, the more laws we have, the more criminals we will create. So, reversing the dominant idea of the role of governance should be the *Laozi*'s primitivist advice – let many spontaneous *dao*s coexist. It expresses the *Laozi*'s faith that a natural order (say of the kind envisioned in Chapter 80) will, in fact, be positive.

CHAPTER 58

GOVERNMENT IN UNCERTAINTY

This chapter starts again overstating its theme – almost as if to say that "bad" government (government that ignores its conventional role) is best because it would allow natural resolutions and harmonies to emerge in the people. Further, we never know the ultimate outcome of our social engineering. Apparent tragedies may turn out to have surprisingly good results – and vice versa. No one knows what comes at the end of the long run. There is no natural standard of what is correct – thus reversal of opposites can work.

What we regard as correct at one time may seem strange at another; doing well may come to seem like sheer coincidence. We can't find an end to such doubts about doing things – so the sage does the opposite. (This is actually a dangerous turn in primitivist political theory, because it excuses ignorance and error.)

CHAPTER 59

CONSERVING AND PREPARING

This chapter develops a more defensible primitivist theme that draws on natural ways. For example, it supports modern ecologists seeking validation in Daoism for their environmental ethics. Conserving 嗇 *se* ("thrifty:miserly") is good both in governing humans and in dealing with nature. Holding in reserve is being ready to respond – and is therefore a constituent of virtuosity. If preserved, what we acquire (in skills especially) can then be utilized to control more situations. And this advantage does not seem to have any limit.

Although the cycle of platitudes found here can be read in ecologically sound ways, the passages can just as easily be (and often were) read as Machiavellian politics. Take your choice.

CHAPTER 60

GOVERNING LARGE STATES

This much beloved passage combines the negative, primitivist advice of the earlier chapters in this sequence on governing with the practical norm of Chapter 59. The analogy 烹小鮮 ("grilling a small fish") works better for fishermen – the secret of governing a large and complex state is not to mess with it much. Using this way of managing the social world is not to attribute to it any special content or *dao* other than "do not harm people". Not merely does our system not harm, "ghosts" (鬼 *gui*) do not become intentionally aware (神 *shen*; so they can't "target" us for harm), or, if we think of "its spirit" as the governing system's spirit, it

will avoid harming humans. Even were we to fail at that goal, we could still use ways and methods to keep sages from harming people. As long as the combined outcome of the institutions and the sages or leaders do not harm humans, then their virtuosities can come into natural balance, returning to the meaningful goal – not harming people.

CHAPTER 61

BEHAVIOUR OF STATES

This theme is ambiguous. We can read it as vaguely reflecting on the use of the concept 下 *xia* ("lower") in state relations. *Xia* ("lower"), like 靜 *jing* ("still"), figures in the procreational *yin–yang* organic model as a *yin* or 牝 *pin* ("female") aspect – passive, receptive, in the lower position. The passage makes identical claims about both big and small states. Each uses "below" on the other and takes it, but the summary inserts a minimal grammatical difference suggesting some unclear contrast. One treats *X* as below *in taking*; one treats *X* as below *and takes*. Interpreters tend to translate the second as a passive verb – the smaller states are taken. This conventional result – the small are taken and the big take them – is not warranted by the grammar, neither does it make a coherent point about reversal. Because taking that stance led to opposite results, it cannot follow that simply taking the lower position leads to your getting on top.

One way to get a coherent, though more abstract, reading is to treat the passage as merely stressing the importance of the *yin* value of "beneath" to all states. Greater ones because they want to "domesticate" the smaller (that is, lower) states and thus "flow down", and smaller ones because they want to survive by being good servants absorbed into greater systems. Thus each state gets what it wants by focusing on "lower" – each takes the other in a different sense. This is an uncharacteristically elitist chapter and probably reflects some Legalist input.

CHAPTER 62

OBSCURE WAYS

This passage reminds us, first, that *dao*s are not natural kinds. Rather, they subtly permeate the structure of 萬物 *wan-wu* ("10,000 natural kinds") – *spaces*, openings for each creature of possible courses of action weaving between and through things in reality. The courses of different things can interact and, conceptuallly, we blend them together. (A course for me, one for you, may interact and conceptually blend into a course for *us*.) In this way, *dao*s of many things blend into an aggregate which *dao*s them all in their interaction. Skilful people value *dao*s, but even unskilful ones seek and follow them. Beautiful language, even if it is not directly practical, is marketable, and fidelity or accuracy in linguistic performance is to everyone's benefit. So we have every reason to be concerned for

those who are not good at things. They constitute a market for those teaching how to perform *dao*s.

The next fragment addresses the Confucian–Mohist model of *dao*-instruction through a hierarchy of authority – topped by a 天 *tian* ("sky:nature") 子 *zi* ("son:master"), which the religious treat as "son of heaven". We can naturalize and neutralize this moralistic reference and describe the same person either as an "offspring of nature" or someone who, by virtue of practically succeeding or having know-how, counts as a master in the natural context. This naturalized description reflects a view shared by Daoists and Legalists: the ruler is neither sagely wise nor morally insightful, merely another natural human in a unique confluence of circumstance. Other passages suggest distancing this model from the conventional trappings of artificial charisma (tributes and pomp) in favour of simply promoting our natural, universal *dao*s. We should follow ancients *who did not follow* ancient authority; they simply found ways to succeed in their context, just as we do. They were not taking their own future decisions (laying down the social norms) as a given moral goal. They were creating morality for themselves. We all find our ways from where we are – even criminals find natural ways to 免 *mian* ("escape").

The result may seem mildly at war with the more common rejection of any attempt to deliberately guide the deeming of the social world (found in chapters 29, 39, 45, and 49). We should understand the result, as we did in Chapter 56, as surrendering teaching and waiting for each to catch on and continue, letting the social world's ways of deeming emerge from a blending of each planning perspective undominated by authority – the autonomy of natural morality.

CHAPTER 63

NOT ACTING ON CONSTRUCTS

This chapter directly confronts some of the paradoxes to be found within the primitivist, anti-language (no deeming and acting using constructs) stance. In the end, we act on the construct of not acting on constructs – 為 *wei* ("deem:do") 無 *wu* ("lack") 為 *wei* ("deem:do").

Isn't recommending dealing with people by not using social patterns of dealing, in fact, using a social pattern of dealing? Primitivist sages recommend an alternate conceptual model for our shared practice. Isn't "bland" or "tasteless" a description of its flavour? The paradox has many other forms, ranging from a *dao* that cannot *dao*; language distorts *dao*; learn not to learn; saying not to use names; knowing not to know; desiring not to have desires, and so on.

Where the contradiction is openly acknowledged, as it is in this chapter, all such paradoxes should be read as heuristics (a description that is not strictly true but which aids reflection that should lead to

greater insight into what is true). Wittgenstein said of his own heuristic, when you understand me, you understand it as nonsense – but helpful nonsense, like a ladder you use to climb up and then kick away.

So what is the plausible point of this "nonsense" heuristic? We may interpret it as appreciating the impracticality of construct absolutes, ideal types that fail to register the inherent complexity of opposites in real contexts. Appreciating this opens us to treating resentment with virtuosity rather than adding our own moral resentment. We appreciate the complexity that reminds us to plan for difficulties while things are easy, and deal with large problems while they are still small.

Wise people can indeed do great things by focusing on small ones. By regarding easy problems as precursors of 難 *nan* ("harder") ones, they make those harder problems 易 *yi* ("easier") to deal with.

The *Laozi*, unfortunately, does not tell us how to predict what the hard shape of something easy will be, or how to act to prevent it. It may be naturalistic, but it's not practical science.

CHAPTER 64

PLANNING AHEAD

This chapter smoothly picks up the commonsense theme. It rehearses the last example from Chapter 63 and elaborates ever more creative versions, culminating in the most famous slogan of Daoist gradu-alism: 千 *qian* ("thousand") 里 *li* ("league: mile") walk starts with 足 *zu* ("foot: sufficient") 下 *xia* ("lower:down"). ["A thou-sand-league walk starts with a footfall."]

The next fragment abruptly revisits the primitivist paradoxes. This is another passage where one wonders if the sages' commentary is from the sages whose absence would benefit us a hundredfold – the self-styled sage of conventional wis-dom; the kind of knowledge we should abolish? As noted above (Chapter 47), "using this, sages. . . " may introduce a way of missing the point of the passage it re-acts to. The hint that sages can somehow avoid the messy negative outcomes by not acknowledging them and reading the ad-vice as self-sabotage at the point of success seems to war with any commonsense use of the heuristic. It suggests the *conventional* sage has taken the paradoxical slogans too literally.

The second sage commentary is remi-niscent of two themes in the *Zhuangzi*. One is that we need not conclude by rejecting all conventions; the conventional is the useful and that is the best touchstone we have to real guidance. The second is that if unmedi-ated intuitive spontaneity is the point, then the sage and the fool are indistinguishable. The fool and the sage both act from their "no-construct guided" nature. Perhaps the sage is merely a lucky fool.

CHAPTER 65
THEORY OF GOVERNING

This chapter most openly invites the Con-fucian charge that the *Laozi* is as concerned to dominate as were Confucians and Mo-hists. However, Laozi does it deceptively – pretending to aim for a lower position in the hope that reversal will place him on top. This passage would have been taken literally by the despotic Legalist thinkers of the Qin who burned books and buried philosophers. Daoists should rebut this charge by citing the merely heuristic role of these 反 *fan* ("reversals") of value. It refers to conventional knowledge and sages, to the alleged Confucian and Mohist "know-ing to" impose a single moral *dao* on the social world. The reversal heuristic should stimulate appreciation of the natural, spon-taneous forms of autonomous guidance. Making people wise 明 *ming* ("discern-ing") in applying conventional names and distinctions is actually making them 愚 *yu* ("stupid") in natural common sense and vice versa. A heuristic reading aligns this chapter with earlier ones which suggested that sages are bad.

So this chapter can be read in two ways: a Daoist leader would make people dull – absent the discrimination of Confucian scholars; a Confucian leader makes peo-ple forget their natural practical wisdom. The second fragment then can start from the insight into the duality of wisdom im-plied by the heuristic. Knowing to reverse traditional guidance is a deep kind of virtuosity – one that allows us to flow with changing nature.

CHAPTER 66

LEADING FROM BEHIND

This chapter reprises the ambiguously stated point about the 上 下 *xiang-xia* ("upper–lower") distinction found in Chapter 61 and extends it to the contrast of 先 後 *xian-hou* ("ahead–behind"). The abstract invitation to value the unconventional one shares all the earlier ambiguity – does the sage desire to be above the subjects or (the active reading) to raise the subjects? Whichever we choose, we seem to have to adopt sequentially both opposing structures. In consideration of Daoism's image of non-assertive benevolence, we alternate to get that result – authoritarians, like Legalists, can reverse the pattern.

His speech could belittle the people or it could belittle himself: for example, the self-description as 孤寡不穀 "the lonely, orphan" versus the Legalist "son of Heaven"; or he puts his being/body behind them in importance – or behind them in the face of danger or battle.

The sage commentary has the sage positioning himself above people. Is it missing the point again? Or is the point a benevolent one – that the subjects do not feel his weight as a burden? That his being in front protects the people?

The flexible interpretation works because, as the chapter ending notes, the sage disagrees with no one, therefore no one disputes with him. Is this cynical or, instead, deeply benevolent?

CHAPTER 67

A DIFFERENT WAY

This chapter sustains a more consistent benevolence, but it continues to express a ruler's ideology. The *dao* which the social world regards as great is the guiding discourse of the *Laozi*. It implies that the only grounds for praising it is its not being "familiar" (肖 *xiao*). However, his "three treasures" turn out to be rather conventional moral (Confucian and Mohist) values of charity, frugality and modesty. After prosaic praise for these virtues, the passage suggests that the main reason for them is the ruler's survival, success in battle, and sustained rule. This Machiavellian view of moral values was a core theme in the Legalism rampant in the Qin/Han era.

CHAPTER 68

SUBTLE ROLE PERFORMANCE

The perspective here shifts from the ruler's point of view to a more military perspective. The military advice reminds us of similar themes in Sunzi's *Art of War*. Both warn against aggressive posturing, advise avoiding engagement, and stress good management of one's armies. We can read these lines as further illustrations of heuristic reversal, but the point is still about war and winning. The pacifism of the early chapters seems forgotten.

CHAPTER 69

WAR AND WINNING

Recall the pacifist reflection in Chapter 31 where we look for the discourse of war in the funeral rite 哀 *ai* ("mourning"). This chapter manages to recover a similar point, but it still takes the point of view of the military leader, advising him on how to achieve success.

However, the advice that is preferred shares themes with the earlier, more anti-war version. Good generals do not acknowledge they have enemies; they do not mass armies or weapons. Still, the context and the intrinsic goal is the ruler-warrior's concern to preserve his life and treasure.

The earlier, poignant image of mourning in funerals is turned to advising the general to avoid battle – especially against an equally matched opponent – as a way to preserve his army and the grief that would ensue from any losses.

CHAPTER 70

UNDERSTANDING ME

The point of view has shifted over a score of chapters, first to rulers, then to military leaders and finally, in this last section, it reflects more gratifyingly on the puzzle of what lesson to draw from the self-defeating heuristic. Its implication is neither easy to understand nor to follow (行 *xing*, "walk").

The passage protests that it is really extremely easy to know and practise, without further explanation. Further, it acknowledges that no one knows or practises it. A favourable way to read this is broadly Nietzschean (and Zhuangzian): the best way to follow what I advocate is not to follow. The will to power is a form of self-creation. Words and practices were created by those who did not have them yet. If we follow them, we too should create in our own context rather than mimic their actions from another context. So not knowing what I'm telling you to do simply amounts to not knowing what to do.

If that is the point of the chapter, it lies hidden behind an analysis that conflicts with one earlier theme – that of not valuing rare stuff. It might be that each of us self-creates something unique, hence rare. However, if that is the point the commentary of the "sage" again misses it, because the sage furtively and selfishly hides his valuable object by wrapping it in a bit of common cloth.

CHAPTER 71

PARADOX AND PRACTICALITY

The sensible heuristic reading of the paradoxes becomes more clear in this chapter. It is not simply that knowing is bad; knowing when not to know is the important point – precisely when it is better to rely on second nature, cultivated intuitions or skill sub-routines that do not occupy conscious processing space, thus freeing that space for higher thought. (One of the senses of 知 *zhi*, or "know", in classical Chinese was "conscious", so sleep was described as "the *zhi* not *zhi*ing".) However, 不 *bu* 知 *zhi* 知 *zhi* ("not to know to know" – when, how, that or what to know) is also a defect.

"Defect" (we normally translate the character 病 as "disease") is a construct. In using it, sages are 病 *bing* ("defecting") 病 *bing* ("defect"); they are "defect"-ing but not defective. This structure is a kind of belief context. It means only that they are deeming *bing* to be *bing*.

The Mohist dialecticians made a similar argument when defending against the charge that their opposition to fatalism was "fated". Using the word "fate" to reject commitment to "fate" did not require accepting fate. (See the discussion of *yi-wei*, page 30.)

CHAPTER 72

ALLEGIANCE AND RESPECT

The increased subtlety and clarity of statement continues, now on the subject of leadership. The upshot is simply avoid cruelty so your subjects will not fear you. This moral is appreciated by the best of Legalist thought – and is distorted or forgotten in the worst. One good argument offered for 法 *fa* ("standard", typically translated as "laws") is that if we have clear standards restricting official use of punishment, then people will fear officials less. People can plan courses of action with less risk of coercive repression. It gives people a way to resist authority by creating legitimate grounds for opposing arbitrary use of official force. This respects people's spontaneity; it allows them more leeway to set their own course in life, at the same time maintaining a stable cooperative social order. So sages should not despise the people's spontaneous, locally and naturally emerging creativity.

Does the sage commentary get it right? This time, it has the merit of being ambiguous. The character for "see" frequently is used as "display" (later, an element added to this character removes the ambiguity). So this can be read as a conventional (and trivial) "do not strut around" or it can be read as knows from here yet sees other points of view – does not "see from here". Loves from here yet does not value only from here but from multiple points of view.

Sages ambiguously mix the traditional inherited posture of objectivity and the importance of local, spontaneous judgment.

CHAPTER 73

TOLERANCE AND NATURAL WAYS

Daoist political theory rarely reflects on the problem of real evil. Primitivism is optimistic – evil is rare. Most of what we call "evil" is people acting from other points of view. However, sometimes acting can become dangerous to others, particularly when we are credulous or 敢 *gan* ("presumptive") about our own special access to truth. Bravery with the presumption that we are correct then leads us to killing. Bravery, but without that presumption, allows both views to coexist. Sometimes bravery is a benefit, sometimes not. If this chapter is a recipe for non-violence, then it is tinged with the wisdom of Old Lodge Skins from *Little Big Man* (1970): "Well, sometimes the magic works, sometimes it doesn't."

There are some things nature itself seems to abhor (惡 *wu*, "hate:ugly") – why do they occur? The sages' solution makes it even harder to know. The natural way is to win without contending, to get the desired response without disputing. Without calling it forth, to have it spontaneously arise. This expresses an optimism, like that of the ancient Greeks, that implicitly we all strive for a harmonious resolution of conflict.

Nature, though not sensing, does seem to have a plan that encompasses all; and while allowing each its own way, lets none slip out.

CHAPTER 74

EXECUTION AND MURDER

If life were intolerable, killing would not work as a threat. If society made life tolerable and then proposed to seize and kill deviants, who would 敢 *gan* ("dare:presume") do it? This is the real issue with capital punishment – not the deviant's right to life, but the executioner's presumption. If society wants to get a really proficient killer, it could use a hit man – they are good at their craft. If society tries to get someone with normal sensibilities to do the killing, it's going to harm them. No one for whom killing is not a way of life can kill without having it damage them in some way.

CHAPTER 75

EATING THE PEOPLE

The economics of the *Laozi* does not envision technology beyond the efficiency that comes from having the land at peace. So the amount of goods is limited and consumption is a zero-sum game. If the aristocracy eats without producing, they must take it from the people who grow the food. The orthodox level of taxation was to take the produce of one field in nine. Overtaxed, the people starve in order to let the upper classes enjoy 生之 *sheng zhi* ("life's") 厚 *hou* ("thickness"). This "thickness", the conception that the rich and privileged have of life, is one that is embellished by their highly cultivated "tastes". These are "thick" learned tastes, not natural ones. We learn them by acquiring the capacity to use clever words such as "bouquet", "aftertaste" and "dry" so that they value only the rare items and not the ordinary.

Reducing people to starvation (as Mencius famously noted) makes them harder to govern. Faced with such a death, they do not fear the executioner – they become rebellious and a threat to your rule.

Do not concentrate on how to live more fully yourself and you'll be better at really valuing life.

CHAPTER 76

TOLERANCE AND FLEXIBILITY

This chapter uses a familiar Daoist idea – things are 柔弱 *rou rou* ("malleable") when young and 堅強 *jian qiang* ("stiff" when old). Strength and rigidity are stations on the way to death. The moral for political and military leaders is that being strong, tough, hard and solid is not for the best. Being able to bend, to absorb, to fight in the Judo (soft-way) or Tai-chi style is the more enduring kind of political and martial skill.

CHAPTER 77

NATURAL AND HUMAN WAYS

The optimistic primitivist reads the cycles of nature as reflections of cosmic justice. It pulls the high part down and fills in the low, pares back surplus and supplies the needy. Perversely, human leaders tend to do the opposite; their less optimistic "realism" tells them that a ruthless market is the law of nature. The rich get richer and the poor get poorer; society taxes the poor while giving handouts and tax breaks to the wealthy. What leader would have the insight to take from the wealthy and give to the poor? Only one with a natural way.

Does the sage commentary get it right? Well, this natural way does have constructs: harmony, balance, justice, fairness. However, if the sage is an optimistic primitivist, he will see this pattern in nature and, when it succeeds, not name or take credit for it. What he does (為 *wei*, "deem:do") fits under the concept of fairness, but not because he relies (恃 *dai*) on it, and he claims no status for achieving it. That's close – it might be wiser to coincide with the concept without being concerned with your status or reason.

CHAPTER 78

REVERSAL OF VALUES

The overall bias in talk about reversal is toward the mild, peaceful, non-assertive values. While not strictly consistent, that bias makes sense as a reversal of the conventional (Confucian and Mohist) emphasis on active, assertive, states and coercive governments. Water appears again to enhance the point: it wins over hard and firm things by conforming to them, by yielding and avoiding confrontation. This is common sense, but people have trouble with it; we are reactive, incline to retribution and enjoy dominance.

The sage commentary says we have to accept apparent wrongs in the state. The conventional discourse about correction works as a discourse treating the opposite things as correct. So the 正 *zheng* ("correct") 言 *yan* ("language:discourse") will be like its 反 *fan* ("opposite").

CHAPTER 79

NATURAL WAYS
OF RECONCILING

We do not need to be perfect in dealing with conflict. Can we still count as being good at reconciling? The sage commentary seems arbitrarily to take a side in agreement (tallies were broken apart so their matching up proved authenticity) but without making a 責 *ze* ("responsibility") claim on the other party. This is virtuosity in supervising agreements, while being lenient about its details. Nature has no special preference – we should focus mainly on being with those who are good at doing their thing.

CHAPTER 80

IDEAL PRIMITIVE
STATES

This celebrated (but vexing) paean to the primitivist village utopia rules out any expansive plans for larger social units. The range of natural sociability is the agrarian village, so shorn of technology it is almost Neolithic. And where it has technology it lacks any tendency to use it. People value their lives and family and revert back to using 結 *jie* ("knotted") 繩 *sheng* ("rope") for counting. People love their food unadorned, live in peace with those around them, and enjoy cultural entertainments; they so lack curiosity that even though they are able to hear the dogs bark and the cocks crow in the next village, they have no desire to visit.

Beautiful as it is, this primitivist conception does not deal with where sons and daughters will find mates. Do primitivists recognize any danger of inbreeding (or taboos) and the attraction to novelty? It does not strictly conform to the anti-language programme – knotted ropes are still symbol systems, even if not verbal or written.

CHAPTER 81
WORDS AND ACTIONS

There is an interesting irony in having this passage come after the beautifully described primitivist utopia. Accurate (信 *xin*, "trustworthy") 言 *yan* ("language:discourse") may not be beautiful and 美 *mei* ("beautiful") words may not be accurate. But the piece does not say what is wrong with the lovely words – including its own, or what we should take this slogan to imply about the whole poem. As usual, it does not make either 辯 *bian* ("distinction dispute") clear. Those who dispute their vision of the utopian village (Confucians and Mohists) are not so good at running societies themselves. Those with conventional knowledge cannot be comprehensive. There are too many points of view to comprehend them all. Those who take the ideal point of view, still can not know what each of us should plan.

Sages do not have their usual "therefore" commentary, but their not seeking wealth should illustrate what to do. In not seeking it for themselves, they act for and enrich others. This amounts to taking everyone's point of view in acting, which, if one does it, makes them sages. If they succeed, they are better off from a cooperative result. Nature, similarly, benefits everyone without harming. Sages act and their actions may correspond to certain social constructs, but they do not use constructs to confront or to contend with others.

ENDNOTES
FOR THE
INTRODUCTION

1 This story grows out of the biographical sketch drawn by Sima Qian in the *Shiji* 史記 (*Records of the Grand Historian*, ca.90–104BC). The Buddhist embellishment dates from the *Laozi Huahu Jing* by Wang Fu (AD290–306).

2 Guo Xiang (see Chronology, page 262) established the classification of Inner, Outer and Miscellaneous, acknowledging the latter two were written after Zhuangzi's death. He averred Zhuangzi may have written some or most of the "Inner Chapters". The *Zhuangzi* style established there was fantasy dialogues between animals, forces of nature, strange creatures, thieves, logicians, and so on. Those chapters had sporadically used Lao Dan and Confucius as speakers in dialogues, possibly based on a legend of Lao Dan having instructed Confucius. The later "Outer Chapters" may have been the first to establish Laozi as a spokesmen for an anti-Confucian philosophy related to Zhuangzi's.

3 See Liu Xiaogan's "Afterword" in his *Classifying the* Zhuangzi *Chapters* (1994), pages 172–186. Liu takes this point as evidence the *Laozi* is older than Confucius.

4 The key elements of the second story presented here are drawn from Angus Graham's argument, which, confirmed by recent archeology, forms the core of most current variations. See Graham (1981), pages 126–128. The Mawangdui silk manuscripts were discovered in 1973 and date from the 2nd century BC. The Guodian manuscripts came to light in 1993 and may be a stem on which the Zhuangist authors grafted their themes. These may have been earlier than the first.

5 The *Shiji* 史記 (*Records of the Grand Historian*) purported to record known history from as far back as the legendary Yellow Emperor more than 2,000 years earlier through to the Han era.

6 The archeological texts hint at this speculative possibility. The Mawangdui, most closely associated with Huang-Lao (see note 7, below), reverses the order so the *De* section comes first. The earlier Guodian selection contains nothing after

Chapter 65 – approximately where the Mawangdui text displaces what in the traditional text are the final two chapters. Although more acute through this later range, the tension between a Machiavellian political and a more philosophical reading pervades the text.

7 The *Hanfeizi* is named after one of Xunzi's students, Han Feizi (ca.280–233BC), who became an advisor to the Qin emperor. An imperial Qin–Han ruler-cult, the Huang-Lao, worshipped Laozi alongside the legendary Yellow Emperor (Huang Di).

8 Other "contexts" for interpretation are not ruled out by this approach. Legalist or Yellow Emperor readings may have been in force when the text was completed. For other reasons, Wang Bi's cosmological Neo-Daoist reading, Buddhist readings, and a wide range of Daoist religious readings reflect more enduring, widespread and causally significant accounts of the "Chinese" meaning than would its meaning to its original philosophical audience, teetering as it was on the brink of being snuffed out by the empire. Although not Chinese, particle physics and hippie readings may also capture what is "true" in the text – viewed from other contexts and background assumptions.

"Text theory" actually flips the traditional story of Daoism on its head: Zhuangzi should be treated as the founder of what is now called "Daoist philosophy" while the *Laozi* should be regarded as expressing insights which support Zhuangism, but from a purportedly more primitive point of view and expressed in a different style (an archaic poetic form), as if it were an earlier inspiration and thereby according it legitimacy by implying more ancient roots.

Note that athough text theory has shifted radically, the traditional account of Daoism still informs most translations – a persistence that can be explained by interpretive theory. Classical Chinese is a dead language – no one learns it the way humans learn a "natural language". Operationally, sinologists take correct interpretation as the one in accord with the current consensus version of that theory and this "state of the art" means that past errors can acquire a stubborn inertia.

9 The technical method of interpretation is a version of holistic "radical" translation (W.V.O Quine and Donald Davidson), using the principle of humanity (Richard Grandy and Simon Blackburn) to evaluate meaning hypotheses and accepting a broadly pragmatic inferential conception of meaning (Wittgenstein, Sellars and Brandom). For more details see Hansen (1992, pages 1–54.)

10 Henry Rosemont and Roger T. Ames express suspicion of treating 義 *yi* ("morality") as morality on these

grounds, and that many of the Western concepts with inferential links to "morality" have no clear counterparts in Confucius's Chinese. They suggest treating it as meaning something more like "appropriate".

While I tend to agree that Confucius's text community neither made that contrast nor gave *yi* the centrality it *should have* had in an ethical theory, I argue it reflects the contrast between concept and conception of *yi*. (See Ronald Dworkin's distinction between concept and conception in "A Special Supplement: The Jurisprudence of Richard Nixon", *The New York Review of Books*, vol.18, no.8, May 1972.)

Someone's theory of morality may permit inferences that another's would not. They may each argue that the meaning of the term entails their theory, but it is best not expect to settle substantive issues by appeal to meaning in this way. The test for meaning is whether objections to a theory are intelligible in the linguistic community; in this case its focus is Confucius and insofar as Confucius has any central role for *yi* (義 "morality") in his thinking, it does not have the centrality the concept of "morality" should have. However, it is doubtful that the lacking inferential links he lists are ones that constitute the concept. They belong to a conception of that concept.

The next thinker in the tradition, Mozi, rejects linking *yi* and established practice and argues it requires an objective, trans-social standard (法 *fa* "standard") to judge social practices as *yi* or not. The *concept* is characterized by the familiar quasi-reality we use to distinguish moral standards from conventional ones. (The link, for example, of liberty and morality is part of a particular theory of morality – ours. It is not a contradiction to speak of a morality that does not value liberty – it's merely an unappealing paternalistic moral theory. It is like the link between "married" and "male and female". In a particular social structure, an inference is highly probable. But if we discover that Frank and Jim are married, our language acquisition device does not self-destruct. It is perfectly intelligible in English to learn that same-sex marriage is legal and even routine.)

The one late passage in the *Analects* that does mention both concepts hints at having appreciated Mozi's analysis – an acknowledgement we find in later Confucian theorists such as Mencius and Xunzi as well.

11 See Robert Eno, *The Confucian Creation of Heaven: Philosophy and the Defense of Ritual Mastery* (Albany: SUNY, 1990).

12 Hall and Ames postulate a contrast between an aesthetic (Chinese) and a logical (Western) order. This is my

own interpretation of the point of that contrast. See David Hall and Roger T. Ames, *Thinking Through Confucius* (Albany: State University of New York Press, 1987, pages 131–137).

13 The normal translation, "virtue", is acceptable if we gloss it in the Aristotelian sense as "excellence". "Virtuosity" is preferred here because of the worry (in my religious upbringing, "virtue" was code for sexual chastity) that familiar Christian moralistic overtones will rupture the crucial conceptual link to the aesthetic model that has been explained. Further, "virtue" does little (without supernatural intervention) to incorporate Arthur Waley's insight that "power" is a component of the meaning of *de* (德 "virtuosity"). Virtuosity explains a power that comes from a reliable ability to executing one's *dao* correctly – hence a virtuoso boxer can beat a muscle-bound bruiser. And those with virtuosity naturally come to be regarded as leaders, role models and teachers.

14 Classical Chinese writers commonly resort to parallelism to resolve ambiguities of parsing which would otherwise plague a language without sentence-role inflection and punctuation.

15 The distinction drawn previously (see note 10), between the concept and conception, is important here. Mozi is clearly using the concept of 義 *yi* ("morality") to express a conception much closer to our sense of "morality" than early Confucians did – that is, of a system of guidance that can legitimately evaluate and criticize other social practices such as mores, etiquette, funeral, religious and even political ritual. Many of Henry Rosemont's other crucial conceptual ties are still lacking, however, including, crucially, reason, autonomy, duty, law, principle, and responsibility. Mozi does have a version of choice but it is a blend of interpretive choice and choice of linguistic *dao*. The utility criterion governs both deciding what moral discourse to share in a society and how to interpret that discourse into performance or behaviour.

16 This character is like the character *bian* (辨 "cut:divide") with the meaning radical dividing the two identical sides changed from *dao* (刀 "knife") to *yan* (言 "language") to "yield" 辯.

17 The exception within Buddhism is Zen (禪 *chan*), which, along with other things, absorbs this aspect of Daoism.

18 See the discussion on rectifying names, page 16.

CHRONOLOGY OF ANCIENT CHINA

ca.50,000BC The earliest wave of emigration leaves Africa, travelling along the coast to reach India. Around 40,000BC a branch enters north China to become the northern genetic strain of modern Han peoples. Other branches spread to Australia, Manchuria and North America.

ca.10,000BC A second, land-based wave from Southeast Asia enters China to form the southern genetic strain of the Han.

ca.7000–5000BC Agricultural cultivation and domestication starts in the river basins of, first, the Middle East and then central China.

ca.5000–ca.1700BC Neolithic pottery, jade and bronze production flourish in China.

ca.1500BC The Shang or Yin dynasty, ancient China's first historically authenticated dynasty, develops bronze work into a high quality art with distinctive styling.

ca.1300BC Earliest surviving inscriptions on oracle bones, the sophistication of which is evidence that writing had existed for some time.

ca.1050BC Shang dynasty overthrown by the Zhou. The overthrow occasioned the construction of the Mandate of 天 tian ("nature:sky") theory espoused by the "Duke of Zhou" whom Confucius venerated. Early Zhou is now called Western Zhou.

ca.770BC Internal revolt disrupts the Zhou succession. Capital moved east to Luoyang, marking the beginning of Eastern Zhou.

770–481BC Spring and Autumn Period; the Eastern Zhou succession continued, weakened by division into de facto independent states. Rulers of these states gradually assumed the title of king (wang).

ca.571–ca.320BC Estimate of dates Lao Dan (Laozi) would have been born and eventually left China to become the Buddha, according to traditional legend.

ca.551–479BC Confucius (Kongfuzi) lived and trained a generation of students in the practices of the 乳 ru (Confucian or Confucianism). His syllabus includes a book of poetry, of history, and of 禮 li (ritual).

453–221BC Warring States Period. Inter-state rivalry breaks into frequent conquest. Later, Confucians start writing the Analects (Lunyu) composed mainly of aphorisms attributed to Confucius.

480–398BC Mozi teaches a fiercely anti-Confucian doctrine, justified on utilitarian grounds. His teachings are recorded in at least three versions by his students. They form coherent, argumentative essays structured in elaborate parallels.

469–399BC Socrates teaches students in Athens until sentenced to commit suicide after a democratic populist trial.

428–348BC Plato uses the Socratic method dramatically to develop his rationalist theory of forms in a series of dialogues with Socrates as the protagonist.

384–322BC Aristotle adapts Plato's teaching into a more naturalistic scheme, developing a proto-science – especially of biology. His rich corpus of lecture notes comprehend all aspects of philosophy from metaphysics to logic, aesthetics, politics and ethics.

ca.350BC Mohist dialecticians, Gongsun Long, Hui Shi and other anonymous thinkers, debate and theorize language, reference, distinctions, and norms for using compounds.

378–291BC Mencius teaches an innatist version of Confucianism to respond to the spread of Mozi's teachings and those of an egoist theorist – Yang Zhu. Mencius's teachings, perhaps at least partially written by him, consist mainly of extended discussions with rulers and other thinkers.

ca.395–315BC Shen Dao, cited as "predecessor" by people associated later with both Daoist and Legalist trends in thought, develops the notion of "The Great *Dao*".

ca.360–300BC Song Xing develops the idea of being locked in a perspective created by social standards of evaluation. He advocates restricting desires to the natural (pre-social) ones, to reduce competition and war. This is similar to the structure in the *Laozi*.

370–301BC Zhuangzi lived; he started the text tradition that becomes the *Zhuangzi*. His most likely teacher and philosophical influence was Hui Shi, a mystically inclined semantic relativist schooled in theory of language. Zhuangzi ridicules Mencius's intuitionism and regularly bests Hui Shi in debate. Rejecting "Great *Dao*" monism, he argues for broad, mild scepticism.

300–240BC Various students of Zhuangzi continue writing in his style, leaning toward primitivist and syncretist ideas, ignoring and eventually repudiating the analytic inputs into his thought.

295–205BC Anonymous authors compile an early version of the *Laozi* in two scrolls which form the 道德經 *Dao-de* (*Daode*) *Jing*.

ca.305–234BC Xunzi lived and tried to construct an authoritarian, pragmatic conventionalist version of Confucian to answer Zhuangzi's criticisms. He also made Laozi a target of criticism.

221BC The state of Qin under the First Emperor completed the conquest of China. Advised by students of Xunzi, he declared an end to "philosophical dispute", burned books and buried scholars – and brought the creative period of thought (the Hundred Schools of Thought) to a shuddering halt. He unified standards for every conceivable dimension, weights, measures, width of chariots, and the writing system. He organized the entire state into martial units. he conscripted thousands to fortify and extend the Great Wall and dig major canals. His superstitious search for long life led to toleration of the Huang-Lao cult with its attachment to the *Laozi*.

280–233BC Hanfeizi (Han Fei), one of Xunzi's students, lived. He advised the emperor to use draconian pre-emptive measures against any potential rival, then he died when the emperor, taking his advice, executed him. The text in his name, the *Han Feizi*, contains the first commentary on the *Laozi*, but its authorship is not known.

207BC Qin dynasty overthrown.

206BC Liu Bang founded the Han dynasty and continued the Qin's bureaucratic system.

186–140BC The Silk Road was opened up to the West. Confucianism favoured as a state cult.

165–110BC Sima Tan lived. He launched a project to write a universal history, from the beginning (The Yellow Emperor) to the Han. After his death the work was continued by his son.

ca.145–86BC Sima Qian lived and completed his father's project, the 史記 *Shiji* or *Records of the Grand Historian*. Father and son, adherents of the Huang-Lao cult, divide the schools of philosophy and create the classifications of Daoist, Legalist and School of Names.

AD25–220 Eastern Han dynasty. Probable introduction of Buddhism to India.

220–581 Period of Disunion.

226–249 Wang Bi compiled the most widely used version of the *Laozi* text, accompanied by his commentary, which a) favours Confucianism and b) combines the ideas of Laozi and the *yin-yang* ideas in the popular divination text, the *Yijing* (*I Ching*).

252–312 Guo Xiang compiles the version of the *Zhuangzi* text that survives as the basis for studying Zhuangist thought. He classifies the chapters into "Inner" (written by Zhuangzi himself), "Outer" and "Miscellaneous" (both written by later followers). Combined with Wang Bi, the renewed focus on "Lao-Zhuang", also known as "Dark Learning", thrives in popular discussion meetings known as "Pure Conversation", which involve Buddhists and pave the road for portraying Buddhist ideas using Daoist concepts. The common features of their cosmological–metaphysical framework for harmonizing Daoism with Confucianism becomes known as Neo-Daoism.

FURTHER READING

Ames, Roger T. and Hall, David L.
Thinking Through Confucius. Albany,
NY: State University of New York Press
(SUNYP), 1987.

Ames, Roger T. and Henry, Jr., Rosemont.
The Analects *of Confucius: a Philosophical
Translation.* New York: Ballantine, 1998.

Blakney, R.B. *The Way of Life: Lao Tzu.*
New York: Mentor, 1955.

Bodde, Derk. *Essays on Chinese
Civilization.* Princeton, NJ: Princeton
University Press (PUP), 1981.

Bokenkamp, Stephen R. *Early Daoist
Scriptures.* Berkeley: University of
California Press, 1997.

Brooks, E. Bruce and Brooks, A. Taeko.
The Original Analects. Princeton, NJ: PUP,
1998.

Capra, Fritjof. *The Tao of Physics.*
New York: Bantam Books, 1975.

Chan, Alan K.L. *Two Visions of the Way:
A Study of the Wang Pi and the Ho-shang
Kung Commentaries on the* Lao-Tzu.
Albany, NY: SUNYP, 1991.

Chen, Guying 陳鼓應. Lao Tzu: *Text,
Notes, and Comments.* San Francisco:
Chinese Materials Center, 1977.

Cook, Scott. *Hiding the World in the
World: Uneven Discourses on the* Zhuangzi.
Buffalo, NY: SUNYP, 2003.

Creel, Hurlee G. *What is Taoism?*
Chicago: University of Chicago Press
(UCP), 1970.

**Csikszentmihalyi, Mark and Ivanhoe,
Philip J.** *Religious and Philosophical
Aspects of the* Laozi. Albany, NY: SUNYP,
1999.

Cua, Antonio S. *Encyclopedia of Chinese
Philosophy,* vol.1. Routledge: New York,
2002.

Feng, Gia-Fu and English, Jane. *Lao Tsu:
Tao Te Ching.* Taiwan: Caves Books, 1972.

Fung, Yu-lan. (Translated by Bodde, D.)
History of Chinese Philosophy. Princeton,
NJ: PUP, 1952.

Graham, A.C. *Disputers of the* Tao:
Philosophical Argument in Ancient China.
Chicago: Open Court, 1989.

Graham, A.C. *Studies in Chinese Philosophy and Philosophical Literature.* Albany, NY: SUNYP, 1990.

Graham, Angus. "Chuang-tzu's Essay on Seeing Things as Equal" in *History of Religions*, vol.7, no.3, pp.137–159, 1969.

Graham, Angus. *Later Mohist Logic, Ethics and Science.* Hong Kong: Chinese University Press, 1978.

Graham, Angus. Chuang-tzu: *the Inner Chapters.* London: Allen & Unwin, 1981.

Hansen, Chad. "Linguistic Skepticism in the *Lao Tzu*" in *Philosophy East and West*, vol.31, no.3, 1981.

Hansen, Chad. *Language and Logic in Ancient China.* Ann Arbor: University of Michigan Press (UMP), 1983.

Hansen, Chad. "Chinese Language, Chinese Philosophy, and 'Truth'" in *The Journal of Asian Studies*, vol.44, no.3, pp.491–519, 1985.

Hansen, Chad. "Mozi: Language Utilitarianism: The Structure of Ethics in Classical China" in *The Journal of Chinese Philosophy*, vol.16, no.1, pp.355–380, 1989.

Hansen, Chad. "Chinese Ideographs and Western Ideas" in *The Journal of Asian Studies*, vol.52, no.2, pp.373–399, 1993.

Hansen, Chad. *A Daoist Theory of Chinese Thought.* New York: Oxford University Press (OUP), 1992.

Harbsmeier, Christoph. *Science and Civilization in China,* vol.7. Cambridge: Cambridge University Press (CUP), 1998.

Henricks, Robert G. *Lao-tzu:* Te-Tao Ching: *A New Translation.* New York: Ballantine Books, 1989.

Ivanhoe, Philip J. "Skepticism, Skill and the Ineffable Tao" in *Journal of the American Academy of Religion*, vol.61, no.4, pp.639–654, 1993.

Ivanhoe, Philip J. *The* Daodejing *of Laozi.* Indianapolis, IN: Hackett, 2002.

Kaltenmark, Max. *Lao Tzu and Taoism.* Stanford: Stanford University Press, 1965.

Kohn, Livia and LaFargue, Michael. *Lao-tzu and the* Tao-te-ching. Albany, NY: SUNYP, 1998.

Kohn, Livia. *God of the* Dao: *Lord Lao in History and Myth.* Ann Arbor: UMP, 1998.

LaFargue, Michael. *Tao and Method: A Reasoned Approach to the* Tao Te Ching. Albany, NY: SUNYP, 1994.

LaFargue, Michael. *The Tao of the* Tao Te Ching: *A Translation and Commentary.* Albany, NY: SUNY, 1992.

Lau, D.C. *Chinese Classics:* Tao Te Ching. Shatin, N.T. Hong Kong: Chinese University Press, 1982.

Lau, D.C. *Lao Tzu:* Tao Te Ching. Baltimore: Penguin Books, 1963.

Liu, Xiaogan. *Classifying the* Zhuangzi *Chapters.* Ann Arbor: UMP, 1994.

Lynn, Richard John. *The Classic of the Way and Virtue.* New York: Columbia University Press, 1998.

Mair, Victor H. *Experimental Essays on Chuang-tzu.* Honolulu: University of Hawaii Press (UHP), 1983.

Mair, Victor H. Tao Te Ching: *The Classic Book of Integrity and the Way.* New York: Bantam Books, 1990.

Möller, Hans-Georg. *The Philosophy of the* Daodejing. New York: Columbia University Press, 2006.

Robins, Dan. *The Warring States Debate about Human Nature.* Hong Kong: University of Hong Kong Dissertation, 2001.

Roth, Harold D. *The Textual History of the Huai Nanzi.* Ann Arbor: Association of Asian Studies, 1992.

Rump, Ariane, with Wing-tsit Chan. *Commentary on the* Lao-tzu *by Wang Pi.* Honolulu: UHP, 1979.

Smullyan, Raymond. *The Tao is Silent.* New York: Harper and Row, 1977.

Wagner, Rudolf G. *A Chinese Reading of the* Daodejing: *Wang Bi's Commentary on the* Laozi *with Critical Text and Translation.* Albany: SUNYP, 2003.

Wagner, Rudolf G. *The Craft of a Chinese Commentator: Wang Bi on the* Laozi. Albany: SUNYP, 2000.

Waley, Arthur. *The way and its power: a study of the* Tao te ching *and its place in Chinese thought.* London: Allen & Unwin, 1934.

Welch, Holmes. *Taoism: The Parting of the Way.* Boston: Beacon Press, 1966.

Wing, R. L. *The Tao of Power: Lao Tzu's Classic Guide to Leadership, Influence and Excellence.* New York: Doubleday, 1986.

Wong, David. "Taoism and the Problem of Equal Respect" in *Journal of Chinese Philosophy,* v.11 n. pp.165–183, 1984.

Young, Rhett and Ames, Roger T. *Lao Tzu: Text, Notes, and Comments.* San Francisco: Chinese Materials Center, 1977.

Zhang Longxi. *Tao and the Logos: Literary Hermeneutics, East and West.* Duke University Press: Durham, North Carolina & London, 1992.

INDEX

ACKNOWLEDGMENTS & PICTURE CREDITS

ACKNOWLEDGMENTS

Heading the list of people to whom I am indebted for inspiration, challenge and support for this translation are Professor Chen Guying from National Taiwan University, who first exposed me to the parsing controversies that have engaged me for forty years; P.J. Ivanhoe, who first fuelled my enthusiasm for computerized concordances to analyze texts and translations; and Victor Mair, who later challenged me for a full translation to sustain my analysis of the *Laozi* in my *A Daoist Theory of Chinese Thought*. Obviously, I have paid special attention to the insights and guidance in their analyses and translations among the hundreds of translations and commentaries in my database. Development of the professional database used in this analysis was partially supported by a grant from the Research Grants Council (RGC) of the Hong Kong Special Administrative Region, China (HKU 7438/07H), brilliantly implemented by Quinn Whiting-O'Keefe of Coromandel, New Zealand. RGC also funded the work of two research assistants, Cathy Carroll and Wilson Ho, at the University of Hong Kong who helped enormously by editing the translations in the database for data integrity as well as helping to enter several other Chinese philosophy texts, which I have used for my conceptual analyses. The managing editor, Christopher Westhorp, has been patient and inspired in pruning the less accessible aspects of my account as well as coordinating the selection of illustrations and the design of the book. The difficulties for the reader that remain are, of course, entirely my responsibility.

PICTURE CREDITS

The publisher would like to thank the following photographic libraries for permission to reproduce their material. Any errors or omissions are entirely unintentional and the publishers will if informed, make amendments in future editions of this book: **AA** The Art Archive, London; **BAL** The Bridgeman Art Library, London; **WFA** Werner Forman Archive, London; **TBM** © Trustees of The British Museum; **V&A Images** © V&A Images Victoria and Albert Museum

Page 1 *Yin, yang* and the eight trigrams (*bagua*), WFA/Private Collection; **2** Taoist temple, Keren Su/Corbis; **3** Jade dragon pendant, 18th–19th century, TBM; **6** The Great Wall at Mutianyu, Angelo

Cavall/Getty Images; **14–15** Rock-cut stairway on the sacred mountain Hua Shan, Shaanxi, where there are several Taoist temples, Frank Lukasseck/Corbis; **23** Hanging scroll, ink on silk, by Fan Ku'an (990–1040CE), AA/National Palace Museum, Taiwan; **36** Zixiao Taoist temple, Keren Su/ Corbis; **39** Bronze decorated mirror (481–221BCE), V&A Images; **40** A Taoist immortal playing a flute in paradise, ink on silk, 19th century, Korea, WFA/Corbis/P'yongyang Gallery, North Korea; **44** Huangshan mountains, Anhui Province, China, Frank Lukasseck/Corbis; **47** An adept ascends to the heavenly paradise, from *A Keepsake from the Cloud Gallery*, ca. 1750/The British Library; **48** Shrine with Zhenwu, the Three Purities, the Jade Emperor, and other Taoist gods, Ming dynasty, 1406, TBM; **51** Clouds over mountains, Keren Su/Corbis; **52–53** Stream flows over rocks, Panoramic Stock Image/National Geographic Stock; **54** *The Nine Elders of Huichang*, a green jade boulder with seals of the Qianlong emperor, Palace Museum, Beijing; **58** Temple roof detail at Wudang Mountains, Keren Su/Getty Images; **62** Two mandarins of the Ming dynasty court, AA/Topkapi Museum, Istanbul; **65** Spiral galaxy in a star field (digital composition), Fry Design Ltd/Getty Images; **66** Icicles by Bob Rowan/Corbis; **69** Mountains, China, Chris Caldicott/Axiom Photographic; **72– 73** Dragon bells at a temple in Yunnan, China, Craft Images/Alamy; **74–75** Tribute being paid to the Qianlong Emperor (reigned 1736–1795), Qing dynasty, China, AA/Palace Museum Beijing; **77** Beijing forest, China, Kate Kunath/Getty Images; **80** Mountain path winding along the cliffs of Huang Shan mountain, Drew Kelly/Getty Images; **83** An 8th-century copy of the earliest painting attributed to Gu Kaizhi (ca.345–406CE), TBM; **84** Snake Nebula, Canada–France–Hawaii Telescope © Canada–France–Hawaii Telescope–J.C Cuillandre/Coelun; **87** Stone bridge connecting mountains, China, Frank Lukasseck/Coribs; **89** *City Gods and Earth Gods*, 1454, RMN/Thierry Olliver; **90** A rider in a mountain landscape, album painting by an unknown artist, WFA/Private Collection, New York; **93** A door in China, Jochen Schlenker/Getty; **96** Colour on silk of Emperor Ch'in Wang Ti (r.221–210BCE) travelling in a palanquin, Bibliotheque Nationale, Paris/Archives Charmet/BAL; **99** Plate decorated with warrior, Musée Guimet, Dist RMN/Martine Beck–Coppola RMN; **102** Blade of grass, Hans Strand/Getty Images; **105** Blue silk-embroidered panel showing a Taoist immortal in paradise (18th century), V&A Images; **109** Chen Hou Chou and a concubine seeking inspiration for a poem, School of Chiu Ying (16th century), AA/British Museum; **111** Wine jar with design of fishes and water plants, Brooklyn Museum of Art, NY/William E. Hutchins Collection/ BAL; **112** Wood (detail), Theo Allofs/Corbis; **116–117** Incense from a temple in Hong Kong, Andrea Pistolesi/Getty Images; **120** Leaf 9 from *Returning Home*, ca. 1695, by Shitao (Zhu Ruoji, 1642–1707), an album of 12 paintings, ink and colour paper, The Metropolitan Museum of Art, from the P.Y. and Kinmay W. Tang Family, Gift of Wen and Constance Fong, in honor of Mr. And Mrs. Douglas Dillon, 1976. (1976.280a-n) Image © The Metropolitan Museum of Art; **123** A bronze bell from the Shang dynasty (1500–1050BCE), Arthur M. Sackler Gallery, Smithsonian Institution, Washington, D.C: Gift of Arthur M. Sackler, S1987.10; **124** *Portrait du vénérable Wen Yi*, RMN/Thierry Ollivier; **126–127** A Qing period (1644–1912) illustration of a Taoist legend, Musée Guimet, Paris, Dist RMN/Ghislain Vanneste; **131**

Young nobleman on horseback, a handscroll painting, ca.1290, by Qian Xuan (1235–1305), TBM; **132** A stairway through the Huangshan, or Yellow Mountain, range, Anhui Province, eastern China, Frank Krahmer/Corbis; **135** Calligraphy by Li Jinxne of the characters "Mo", for Mo Zi the 5th-century BCE disciple of Confucius, and "Zhuang", for Zhuangzi, the 4th-century BCE Taoist philosopher, WFA/ Private Collection, Sydney; **139** Leaves, Jim Richardson/Corbis; **142** The Sovereign of the Clouds of Dawn, or Heavenly Immortal of the Eastern Peak (Mount Tai), painted silk scroll, ca.1600, RMN/ Thierry Ollivier; **145** A robe with elemental dragons, V&A Images; **146–147** Filial piety, 12th-century Chinese painting, National Palace Museum Taiwan/AA; **149** *The Birds and the Flowers*, cut silk tapestry, or *kesi*, from the Song dynasty, National Palace Museum Taiwan/AA; **150** Seed cup of the sacred lotus, *Nelumbo Nucifera*, Chris Hellier/Corbis; **153** Taoist ritual sword, Ming era, Staatliches Museum für Völkerkunde, Munich; **157** *The Yonzheng Emperor's Nephew at a Daoist Ceremomy for the Recovery of his Father*, a hanging scroll, ink and colours on silk, attributed to Jiao Bingzhen (1689–1726), Qing dynasty, Arthur M. Sackler Gallery, Smithsonian Institution, Washington, D.C: Purchase-Smithsonian Collections Acquisition Program, and partial gift of Richard G. Pritzlaff, S1991.99; **158–159** Taoist temple at Mount Wudang, Hubei Province, Keren Su/Getty; **160** *Emperor T'ai Tsung* (598–649), National Palace Museum Taiwan/AA; **163** Waterfall Robert Y. Ono/Corbis; **164** Divinities, from Taoist book *Great Generals of the Deserts*, (1454), RMN/Richard Lambert; **167** Spider's web, Panoramic Images/Getty images; **170** Chinese painting showing virtue of filial piety (12th century), National Palace Museum Taiwan/AA; **173** Mist in a canyon of Zhangjiajie, Hunan, John Wang/Getty Images; **176** Close-up of a boulder, Micha Pawlitzki/Corbis; **178–179** *Mongol troops of the Emperor of China*, colour on paper (1293), attributed to Tosa Magataka and Tosa Nagaaki, AA/Laurie Platt Winfrey; **182** *The three deities of heaven, earth, and water*, gold on indigo paper, Ming dynasty, dated 1470, Museum of Fine Arts, Boston, Asiatic Curator's Fund and Frederick L. Jack Fund, 1996.58, Photograph © Autumn 2009 Museum of Arts, Boston, from Taoism book *Illuminated Manuscript of the Marvelous Scripture* (1470), Museum of Fine Arts, Boston; **185** *Buildings on a rocky promontory by a lake*, a fan mounted as an album leaf, ink and colour on silk, atributed to the court artist Yan Ciping (12th century), Freer Gallery of Art, Smithsonian Institution, Washington, D.C: Gift of Charles Lang Freer, F1909.245u; **186–187** Taoist temple on Hua Shan, Shaanxi, Frank Lukasseck/Corbis; **191** *Taotie*-decorated ancient axehead, TBM; **192** Aerial view of paddy fields, Frank Krahmer/Corbis; **195** Snow and beech tree, Staffan Andersson/Getty Images; **198** Water and stones, Micha Pawlitzki/Corbis; **201** *A man and two cranes under a plum tree*, album leaf, ink and tint on silk (possibly Qing dynasty), Freer Gallery of Art, Smithsonian Institution, Washington, D.C: Gift of Charles Lang Freer, F1911.162a; **202** Painting on silk of Emperor Yang Ti (560–618CE), AA/Bibliothèque Nationale Paris; **205** Tea-sipping under willows, album leaf, colour on silk (Qing dynasty, 1644–1911), Freer Gallery of Art, Smithsonian Institution, Washington, D.C: Gift of Charles Lang Freer, F1909.247e; **206** Stone-cut engraving of the five original sacred mountains and the four directions around a central mountain, Alamy Images/Die Bildagentur der Fotografen GmbH.